RODNEY WILLIAMSON

The Writing in the Stars

A Jungian Reading of the Poetry of Octavio Paz

UNIVERSITY OF TORONTO PRESS
Toronto Buffalo London

Toronto Buffalo London
Printed and bound by CPI Group (UK) Ltd, Croydon, CR0 4YY

ISBN 978-0-8020-9084-3

Printed on acid-free paper

University of Toronto Romance Series

Library and Archives Canada Cataloguing in Publication

Williamson, Rodney, 1948–
The writing in the stars : a jungian reading of the poetry of Octavio Paz / Rodney Williamson.

(University of Toronto romance series)
Includes bibliographical references and index.
ISBN-13: 978-0-8020-9084-3
ISBN-10: 0-8020-9084-2

1. Paz, Octavio, 1914–1998 – Criticism and interpretation.
2. Jung, C.G. (Carl Gustav), 1875–1961. 3. Archetype (Psychology) in literature. I. Title. II. Series.

PQ7297.P285Z969 2006 861′.62 C2006-904848-7

The author wishes to express his special thanks to Marie José Tramini for her kind permission to quote her late husband's poetry in the original.

This book has been published with the help of funds from the Research and Publications Committee of the Faculty of Arts, University of Ottawa.

University of Toronto Press acknowledges the financial assistance to its publishing program of the Canada Council for the Arts and the Ontario Arts Council.

University of Toronto Press acknowledges the financial support for its publishing activities of the Government of Canada through the Book Publishing Industry Development Program (BPIDP).

This book is dedicated
To Octavio Paz, the man, and Mexico's greatest poet
To my father, and to all who wish to read Octavio Paz in languages beyond his own
To Irene, my wife and significant other, for her love

Contents

THE WRITING IN THE STARS:
A JUNGIAN READING OF THE POETRY OF OCTAVIO PAZ

Prelude

The very conception of this book is predicated on the possibility of distinguishing two basic modes of human thought: a rational, fact-oriented kind, which seeks to establish essentially linear connections of causality and consequence, and a symbolic, associative kind, which establishes networks of meaning by relating images and metaphors. The latter engages what we call the imagination and is the stuff of both poetry and sacred or religious thought. The possibility of distinguishing the two does not imply that they are normally dissociated in the practices of real life. Indeed, they are very often interrelated in thought processes, with either creative or disastrous consequences. However, in given social rituals and, in the longer view of history, even in whole social structures, one or the other will be clearly predominant. The hierarchy of theocratic societies is sustained by symbolic thought. So powerfully did it hold sway in Meso-America, for example, that it survived right up to the fall of the Aztec empire. The last Aztec king lived in a world of omens, portents, and terrestrial and earthly correspondences, in which gods walked the earth in the form of men. In these societies, fully fledged writing systems (systems of signs in our modern sense) could never develop. Systems of 'written' communication could never divest themselves of their symbolic underpinnings and the few indigenous 'books' or codices which survived the Spanish conquest are ideogrammatic architectures, poetry in pictures, rather than linearly ordered messages.

In our western culture, first demythologized by its founders, the Greeks, and in which the rational 'scientific' mode has dominated our thought processes, at the very least since the eighteenth century, it is easy to forget the shifting, dynamic nature of symbolic thought. In symbolic systems, meaning is dependent upon individual acts of enunciation. A symbol 'means' each time it is enunciated in some act of discourse, and each time it will mean something general and something particular, and the boundary between the two will be almost untraceable. In other words, each time the 'same' symbol will mean something different. The enunciation of its meaning is a celebration, a ritual, whose existence depends upon its very enactment. By way of contrast, our modern culture is dominated by supposedly arbitrary signs – words, icons – to which we have at least the illusion of attributing a fixed sense. For the sake of rational argument, we find it necessary to assign meanings to individual words, which in some capacity are independent of their context and static enough to be defined in dictionaries. So accustomed are we, in the modern world, to the constant barrage of explicit messages that we must often work hard to understand the less explicit symbolic ones, such as dreams, innuendoes, and images which inexplicably strike us.

Our concern, in this book, is primarily with the symbolic mode of thought, as we call to witness one of its most prominent practitioners and one of its greatest analysts in the twentieth century. Chronologically, the practitioner, Octavio Paz, bestrides both halves of the century. The work of the analyst, Carl Jung, belongs fairly and squarely to the first half, but his ideas have continued to inspire scholars in a variety of fields, as well as to be developed and broadened in their applications in the current or movement known as archetypal psychology. In the interest of exploring the poetic processes involved in Paz's major poems, we seek to establish a dialogue between Paz and Jung, a dialogic exegesis of the poetic text.

The dialogue between the two will inevitably lead us to a psychological interpretation of the poetic text, given that Jung, for obvious reasons, was interested in commenting on symbols and symbolic thought as psychical projections. Such a view will be found by some to be too one-sided or limiting, though we ourselves could never find it so by virtue of Paz's and Jung's profound knowledge of both eastern and western thought, as well as their tremendous breadth of reference to different cultures throughout space and time, to which their work bears witness. Indeed, it is the rich potentiality of Jung's ideas for the exploration of culture that led to the liberation of archetypal psychology from the constraints of clinical analysis in a way in which neo-Freudian schools and trends have at best been only partially able to achieve. Archetypal psychology, which received its name from a seminal 1970 article by James Hillman, had from the very start 'the intention of moving beyond clinical inquiry within the consulting room of psychotherapy by situating itself within the culture of Western imagination. It is a psychology deliberately affiliated with the arts, culture and the history of ideas, arising as they do from the imagination. The term "archetypal," in contrast to "analytical" which is the usual appellation for Jung's psychology, was preferred not only because it reflected "the deepened theory of Jung's later work which attempts to solve psychological problems beyond scientific models" (Hillman, 1970); it was preferred more importantly because "archetypal" belongs to all culture, all forms of human activity, and not only to professional practitioners of modern therapeutics' (1983, p. 1). And again, in the words of another major exponent, Paul Kugler: 'The major move of archetypal psychology is that it places itself in a poetic tradition and essays a psychology of the imagination, a psychology that originates neither in cerebral physiology, nor in ego psychology, nor in behavioral analysis, but in the workings of the poetic imagination. Archetypal psychology assumes a poetic and mythological basis of mind' (1982, p. 13).

Archetypal psychology, then, situates Jungian thought fairly and squarely in the domain of interest to us here, namely, the poetic imagination, and we shall have occasion to refer to it as we evoke Jungian ideas to illuminate Paz's poetic process. Another prominent Jungian we shall involve in the dialogue is one of Jung's most gifted pupils, Erich Neumann, who directed his attention to the study of consciousness, rather than the unconscious. We shall quote him as an effective complement to Jung's own writings, a voice in consonance with the master's own.

We hasten to say, though, that we have no illusion of presenting any more than one particular view of Paz's poetry. Indeed, it is our contention that any poetic commentary is only a particular reading and can have no claim to be more 'comprehensive' or 'definitive' than others. This is because a poem is not, in fact, 'about' anything, since its liberty of language will always evoke a multiplicity of meanings (unless, that is, it is so bad as not to merit the name!).[1] While one might concede the possibility of 'definitive' readings of novels, the same may not be said of poetic discourse. The great Russian philosopher and aesthete, Mikhail Bakhtin, of course, did much to explode this possibility in his study of novelistic polyphony; he might well have devoted more attention to poetry as the perfect dialogic space.

In undertaking the present study, we have the advantage of the significant number of important studies which already exist on the life and work of Octavio Paz. Especially since the publication of *Piedra de sol*, over the decades scholars have devoted constant critical attention to the poetry of Octavio Paz. It would be illusory and pretentious to suppose that our study could transcend or move beyond their viewpoints, or that in any sense it might give a more complete view of Paz's poetry than others to date. It quite simply continues a line of critical enquiry which has been present in bibliography on Paz since Rachel Phillips's groundbreaking work *The Poetic Modes of Octavio Paz* (1972), but it gives a different, and hopefully richer, perspective on that line of enquiry, because it refers to aspects of the work of Carl Jung that have not traditionally been invoked by Latin-American literary criticism. At this point, we hasten to mention our debt to Richard Callan, a pioneer in Jungian studies of Latin-American literature. His seminal 1977 article, modestly titled 'Some parallels between Octavio Paz and Carl Jung,' was a valuable point of reference for the beginnings of this book. Though concentrating on *El laberinto de la soledad*, it summarizes Jungian concepts applicable to Paz's work as a whole, while proving especially relevant to *Piedra de sol* which, as we shall see, reflects poetically many of the main ideas of *El laberinto de la soledad* (*The Labyrinth of Solitude*).

Given the extensive critical bibliography already devoted to Paz's poetry, the reader may wonder whether yet another study is either desirable or useful. Such an objection presupposes the pursuit of novelty as a guiding principle of literary criticism, rather than seeing it as an accumulation of voices ideally in dialogue with each other, which is the viewpoint to which we adhere. Indeed, the fact that Paz has been one of Latin America's most studied poets offers, to our mind, the advantage of a firm basis on which to construct the close textual commentary around which we will set our dialogue of Paz and Jung in motion.

The reader may further ask why, in these times of postmodernist decentralization, deconstruction, parody, and multiplicity of perspective, we turn our attention precisely to two of the twentieth century's greatest exponents of the unifying, 'universalizing' force of myth.[2] Our book is 'untimely' in the sense that two figures of this stature, while inhabiting their own chronotopic identity, inevitably also transcend their time. It is interesting to note, though, that current fashions have hardly stemmed the flow of critical studies on Paz in the decade of the 1990s and the early years of the twenty-first century, and that no other Mexican poet continues to evoke such abiding interest. Similarly, some may take issue with our reference to Carl Jung rather than to currently more fashionable figures in psychoanalytic thought. An easy response might be that Jung has been a constant source of reference for criticism of Paz's work since its inception. A more elaborate answer might seek to express dissatisfaction with the perceived individualistic limitations of neo-Freudian thought by reviving the essential notion of depth psychology: Jung's 'collective unconscious.'[3] It is the link that Paz and Jung seek to establish at every turn between the psychology of the individual and the psychology of the community and of humankind in general which constitutes the essential affinity between them and thereby our main justification for bringing them together in this book.

It is the 'collective unconscious' which is typically the focus of the few references that Paz makes to Jung in his writings, as, for example, in a short early essay from 1943 entitled 'El auge de la mentira': 'With respect to Plato's theory on reminiscences and archetypes, a notable forerunner of Jung's doctrine of the collective unconscious, can we not say that it is the first, and clearly successful attempt to explain the myths of the poets not as pure falsehood but as hidden truths, as figurative expressions of unconscious and supra-personal memory?'[4]

As will be evident from this quotation, it is not Jung's thought per se which claims Paz's attention.[5] His concern is with poetry, though poetry always in relation to mythology, for mythology is not only the stuff of poetry: poetry also has an essential role as a creator, or a medium of creation of mythology, a role expounded by Paz in a 1942 essay entitled 'Poesía y mitología. El mito' (1988, 271–81). While it is true that the great poets of western golden ages, such as Garcilaso de la Vega, extensively used past myths taken from the western classical tradition (Paz quotes the whole of Garcilaso's sonnet on Daphne's conversion into a tree) (p. 272), it is also true for Paz that modern Man continues to manifest his need for myth. Has 'this thirst for transforming instinctive thought into supernatural forces, for satisfying the darkest appetites by disguising them in fantastic form' (p. 273)[6] disappeared, he asks, from the modern soul? He answers immediately:

> The need for myths has not disappeared; there has just been a change in human consciousness and the mental space of imaginative credulity ... Mankind is no less credulous than when it believed in metamorphosis; it is just that nowadays it believes in different ways about different things. And while it is true that mankind has not relinquished its credulity and need for myths, even if they are called nowadays by other names, it is also nonetheless true that it still possesses the power of imagination it needs to create and understand them. I will try to describe how poetry, that is, creative imagination, has always produced myths to satisfy the man's thirst for pro-

> jection into the realm of the supernatural. And to do that we will have to look closely for a while into the meaning and definition of the word 'myth.' And I have to say very much the same about the word 'poetry.'[7]

It is interesting to observe how Paz moves, in this passage, from the traditional rationalistic 'red herring' of belief and credulity with respect to myth, to the central issue: human creative imagination as an enduring source of mythical production. Incidentally, we would do well to remember the moment in which this was written, when myth was the domain of anthropology, whether from the pioneering turn-of-the-century perspective of Sir James Frazer and the Cambridge School or from the twentieth-century perspective of Malinowski, but in any case before the work of Joseph Campbell and Northrop Frye and before interest in mythology in relation to literature became commonplace.

Jung, for his part, speaks repeatedly throughout his work of the same creative principle under the name of 'active imagination,' which he often relates to dreams and to processes of psychic unification. In his famous 1930 essay 'Psychology and Literature' ('Psychologie und Dichtung'), whose original title would be more accurately translated as 'Psychology and poetic composition,' we may compare the following passage with the one just quoted from Octavio Paz: 'From the very beginnings of human society we find traces of man's efforts to banish his dark forebodings by expressing them in a magical or propitiatory form. It is therefore to be expected that the poet will turn to mythological figures in order to give suitable expression to his experience. Nothing would be more mistaken than to suppose that he is working with second-hand material. On the contrary, the primordial experience is the source of his creativeness, but it is so dark and amorphous that it requires the related mythological imagery to give it form. In itself it is wordless and imageless, for it is a vision seen "as in a glass, darkly." It is nothing but a tremendous intuition striving for expression' (1984, pp. 96–7). The question of belief in these mythological forms is elucidated in his last great book, *Mysterium coniunctionis*: 'you cannot, artificially and with an effort of will, believe the statements of myth if you have not previously been gripped by them. If you are honest, you will doubt the truth of the myth because our present-day consciousness has no means of understanding it. Historical and scientific criteria do not lend themselves to a recognition of mythological truth; it can be grasped only by the intuitions of faith or by psychology' (1963, p. 528).

Another recurring word in Jung's commentaries relating to myth is 'intuition,' a key word in Jungian thought since its identification as one of the four basic psychological functions in Jung's first major book, *Psychological Types* (1921). This ties myth fairly and squarely not only to a non-rational, psychological mode (thinking and feeling are, for Jung, the only psychological functions related to rationality), but also to the unconscious: 'I define sensation as perception via conscious sensory functions, and intuition as perception via the unconscious' ('A Psychological theory of types,' 1971, p. 538).

Paz, on the other hand, like the extraverted individual he is, speaks more of the instinctive (that is, in Jungian terms, the part of the psyche related to sensation). Yet, as we shall see, Paz's poetry in general has as much to do with time, linked to intuition,[8] as it has with the construction of an immediate space, linked to sensation. In fact, from Paz's point of view there is little sense in separating the two, since the present is always presence, and every poetic present contains a nostalgia for its origins, the time and place of the Edenic paradise, and a potentiality for the future. Both Paz and Jung agree, though, in identifying myth and poetry with the non-rational functions of the psyche and with the intersection of the individual with the collective. For Jung, 'the work of the artist meets the psychic needs of the society in which he lives' (1984, p. 104). While for Paz poetry as art is the path along which the poet can move from solitude to communion, and the poetic act as communion is a mainstay of his *ars poetica* from his earliest period.[9] For both Jung and Paz, the collective function of poetry and art lies in its reconciliation of contradictory opposites. Jung states that 'every creative person is a duality of contradictory qualities. On the one side he is a human being with a personal life, while on the other he is an impersonal creative process ... he is "collective man," a vehicle and moulder of the unconscious psychic life of mankind' (1984, p. 101). Paz views this union with the other, with the collective, as the ecstatic discovery of the secret force of the world, a discovery which is at once spiritual and carnal and which can be represented in the figure of the act of love between man and woman:

> In the communion in which the poet discovers the secret force of the world ... Must we say that this force, alternating between the sacred and the accursed, is the force of extasis and vertigo, which surges forth as a kind of fascination at the climax of carnal or spiritual contact? At the height of this contact or the depths of this vertigo, man and woman attain a moment of completeness, in the realm of the harmony of opposites, where life and death commune in a meeting of lips. At that moment body and soul are

> one, and the skin becomes a new form of consciousness, a consciousness of the infinite, reaching towards infinity. The sense of touch and all others cease to function at the service of pleasure or knowledge, they cease to be personal; they *move beyond themselves,* so to speak, and far from being the divining rods or instruments of consciousness, they dissolve it into total oneness, blend it back into primal energy.[10]

Substitute here the word *unconscious* for 'infinite' or 'infinity,' and the thought is entirely Jungian. Paz's initial poetic quest is for the union of opposites, the transcendence of rational (and we might add individualistic) expression in the poem. This is both a formal quest (sometimes seeking the equilibrium of the strictest poetic form) and an intuitive search for a 'nueva conciencia,' which is both a new conscience and a new consciousness which will eventually lead him along the paths of surrealism and thence to the formulation of his theory of 'la otra orilla' (the other shore). The 'other shore' is a dimension outside finite existence attainable through the inspiration of poetry.

The first step towards communion and the union of opposites is a dialogue between the subject and the other, formulated in Paz's early poetry as a dialogue between the poetic 'I' (yo) and a 'you' (tú). Therefore, this will be the point of departure in our exploration of Paz's poetry and the initial topic of our first chapter.

The definition of a starting point in Paz's poetic search and in our particular reading of Paz's poetry presupposes some conception of the overall development of this poetry, which, unfortunately, since April 1998, we can regard as a finished whole. Paz himself assigned considerable importance to the concept of an overall development, as we can see from an interview with Guillermo Sheridan just seven months before his death. In late 1997 the first volume of his collected poetic works *Obra poética I,* had just appeared, and, in reply to Sheridan's question about the rather exceptional process of a writer's editing his own complete works, he made the following comment: 'what I wanted to produce as a writer are works, not just verbal explosions, but works with a structure, with a purpose, with a direction.'[11]

It would, of course, be impossible in a single book to refer to every poem included in the anthologies of Paz's collected poetry (principally those published by Seix Barral and the Círculo de Lectores-Fondo de Cultura Económica). Such an approach would attempt to trace a path through a collection of 'relámpagos, revelación del instante' (lightning flashes, revelations of the instant), as the poet himself describes his shorter poems. Faced with the abundance and richness of Paz's poetic work and its recurring themes, some critics and commentators, such as Pere Gimferrer and John Fein, have adopted the strategy of identifying Paz's longer poems as landmarks in his development. If the short poems are momentary formulations of the instant, the longer ones are about time and thereby justifiably important in the appraisal of the developmental process. Gimferrer traditionally refers to *Piedra de sol* (1957), *Blanco* (1967), and *Pasado en claro* (1974) as representative of the three major stages of Paz's poetry, a point of view he maintains as recently as his tribute to Paz at his death (1998, pp. 11–12). Paz himself, questioned in an interview about Gimferrer's classification, indicates his agreement but adds a fourth poem, 'Carta de creencia,' in what may be a somewhat tongue-in-cheek, but also serious, philosophical reflection on the cardinal points: 'I do not know how important those poems [the ones alluded to by Gimferrer] really are, but they do indeed represent three stages in my life. I would add one more that I wrote later: 'Carta de creencia.' So there are four main poems. I like the number four because it reminds one of the four horizons, the cardinal points. That is a geometric figure, which was very popular with the ancient Indo-American cultures and which has a point in the centre. There are never just two but four suns and, in the centre, a moving sun. The moving sun could be in this case the instant, the poetic instant, the short poems.'[12] Paz here calls into question a linear vision of his work. He invokes the Aztec creation myth of the five suns as a figure of his overall poetic creation: each moment in time, his longer poems, revolves around a common dynamic centre: the poetic instant.

Enrico Mario Santí, in the epilogue to his edition of *Archivo Blanco* (1995) speaks, for his part, of the 'five arms' of Paz's poetry: '*Blanco* is the most ambitious of Octavio Paz's poetic creations, if not the most important. It constitutes one of the "five arms" – together with *Piedra de sol* (1957), *Nocturno de San Ildefonso* (1974), *Pasado en claro* (1974), and *Carta de creencia* (1987) – of the "delta" of five big poems in his work.'[13] For our part, without wishing to fall into the trap of seeing Paz's poetry as a chronological progression, we shall also take these longer poems as convenient points of reference, though we cannot resign ourselves to limiting our view just to Santí's five. *Vuelta*, in our view, merits its place alongside *Nocturno de San Ildefonso* and *Pasado en claro*, and our first chapter will explore Paz's formative period in *Libertad bajo palabra*, the first of his books of poetry considered important by the author himself. In many ways, it is a necessary prelude to *Piedra de sol*. This approach still leaves out many important poems in *Salamandra* (1962) and *Ladera este* (1969), as well as *El mono gramático* (1970), which we have some difficulty in including among Paz's poetic works. The only excuse we offer for our omission is that *Blanco* (1966) is such a watershed in Paz's poetry that it encompasses most of the objectives pursued in his other poetry of the 1960s, as well as enunciating aesthetic tendencies and philosophical viewpoints that mark his poetry of the 1970s and even of the 1980s.

To avoid a tedious overabundance of references and quotations, we assume that the reader is familiar with both Paz's works as well as the major critical bibliography on them. It should be obvious that all of the poems we comment on have received considerable previous attention: we make reference to previous studies only where it seems pertinent to do so. Furthermore, we limit our attention to Paz's poetry, citing his other work, despite its abundance, only in ancillary fashion. We also assume some familiarity with the work of Carl Jung, to the extent that it seems unnecessary to us to offer an introduction, here, to his major ideas. Leticia Underwood does so, in part, in her book *Octavio Paz and the Language of Poetry* (1992), and the reader may also profitably consult introductions to Jungian thought such as Anthony Storr's book *Jung*, or *Man and His Symbols*, a collective work by several Jungians, with an introduction by Jung. In our view, though, there is no better introduction to Jungian thought than the books and essays written by Jung himself, and at appropriate points we give key references to them.

Finally, we add a brief note concerning translation. Translations from Spanish of quotations from Octavio Paz and his critics are, in virtually every case, our own. They are given to help the text to flow more easily and for practical purposes of understanding, with no pretensions of elegance or authoritative precision. The poetry of Paz, though, is quoted in the original, and only gist translations are given below them, for purely practical purposes, with no claims to even remotely reflect the originals' richness of meaning. Given their easy availability, the major English translations of Paz's poetry by Eliot Weinberger, Elisabeth Bishop, Charles Tomlinson, and others are not reproduced here, and the anglophone reader is referred to them in the References section. To have included them would have inevitably begged intertextual commentary, which would have deviated from our purpose. Page numbers for the poems quoted refer to the two major editions of Paz's collected poetry, which we have already mentioned: we chose to reference pages not only to the definitive version of Paz's *Obra poética*, published as Volumes 11 and 12 of his Collected Works by the Fondo de Cultura Económica

(1997, 2003a), but also to *Poemas,* the earlier Seix Barral edition of his poetry from 1935 to 1975 (1979a), complemented by *Árbol adentro* (1987a) for his poems after that date. This is because the most recent volumes of the Collected Works are still not as widely available as they should be outside Mexico. The above editions are referred to respectively by the abbreviations OP1, OP2, SB, and AA.

We hope that these limitations and specifications will serve to make our brief study more, rather than less, readable.

Phase One

Libertad bajo palabra: The Dialogue with the Other

Introduction

The first poetic phase we describe is that of Paz's early poetry from the 1930s onward, leading up to *Piedra de sol*, his first major poem, in 1957. To characterize it as a phase, we see it as dominated and directed by the dialogue between an 'I' (yo) and a 'you' (tú). This is not to say that other views are not possible. Guillermo Sheridan's excellent 2004 biography has done much to fill in the wealth of detail necessary for an appreciation of the Paz of this period as a revolutionary, socially committed poet.[1] But the dialogue between Paz and Jung that we wish to establish leads us to pay close attention to the personal, introspective dialogue in Paz's poetry between the conscious subject and the other, situated by definition outside the subject's consciousness and significantly, in the case of Paz, in the realm of the unconscious. Paz thus establishes a ritual of paradox in poem after poem, in which the quest for the other is closely identified with the process of poetic creation.

In Jungian terms the 'yo'–'tú' dialogue is the necessary pre-condition for the union of opposites, of subject and object, consciousness and the unconscious, which leads, according to Jung, to fullness of being and the construction or enrichment of what he calls the self, which he referred to as the process of 'individuation' (1959a, chap. 6). As Richard Callan puts it: 'For Carl G. Jung, the fullness of being, wherein tensions are resolved and opposites fused into unity, is in fact the archetypal goal of life, and his theories explain both the reason for our solitude and dualism, and the means of approaching wholeness (individuation process)' (1977, p. 916). Since the self is born of the integration of unconscious elements with the conscious ego, its construction necessarily implies an encounter with the unconscious, which for Jung happens at two levels. First, there is the personal unconscious, where the ego's counterpart is the shadow, a centre of unconscious projections which determine to a considerable degree the individual's course in life. Secondly, for Jung's depth psychology there is the level of the collective unconscious, inhabited by archetypal forms. The main ones we are concerned with are the 'anima,' the unconscious female side of man, and the mandala. Yet others occur in the early poetry of Paz. Poetically, the unity of this phase is defined by the verbal expression of recurring archetypes.

Since archetypes reside in the collective unconscious 'identical in all men' (Jung 1959a, p. 4), they can be characterized as 'primordial types ... universal images that have existed since the remotest times' (p. 5). Essentially, they are forms of unconscious content which take on specific characteristics in the individual consciousness in which they happen to appear. They are not summoned at will into conscious thought; rather, they are the agents of a powerful, inexplicable, and intuitive fascination, speaking with 'a voice that is stronger than our own,' since 'whoever speaks in primordial images speaks with a thousand voices; he enthralls and overpowers, while at the same time he lifts the idea he is seeking to express out of the occasional and the transitory into the realm of the ever enduring' (Jung 1984, p. 82).

For Paz, this exploration of the objective, unconscious 'tú' is identified with the creative impulse and the whole process of imagination. This openness to the creative unconscious is, in our view, a major reason for his attraction to surrealism. The influence of surrealism on the arts and literature of Mexico and in Latin America in general has been enormous, of course, much greater than in the English-speaking world. Nevertheless, we should not forget that Paz is one of its major Latin-American exponents, and as such he traces his own path through the surrealist aesthetic. As we attempt to show, the surrealist path of Octavio Paz is a search for new understanding through the unconscious, a search for enriched conscious clarity through grappling with the unconscious.[2] In this respect, Paz differs over many points with André Breton and other European surrealists. Though we do not deal in detail with the relationship between Paz and Breton, since other critics such as Wilson (1980) and Ulacia (1999) have already explored the subject in depth, we have occasion to refer to it below.

To speak of Paz's early poetic production as a single phase implies, no doubt, a certain degree of simplification, since it spans a period of profound development from the early poetic experiments of *Bajo tu clara sombra* and *Calamidades y milagros*, comprising a diversity of short poems in which Paz explores different forms and ideas, to works where Paz has clearly found his voice as a professional poet and is fully involved with surrealism, as in *Semillas para un himno* and *¿Aguila o sol?* It is clear that Paz's travels to Spain, France, and the United States, and his contacts particularly with his French and Spanish poetic contemporaries led to a radical new sophistication in his poetry from the 1940s onward. To justify treating the poetry produced over this period as a single block, it is not enough to point out that Paz himself treated it as such by collecting it under a single title, *Libertad bajo palabra*, published first in 1949, in an extended version in 1960, and reproduced with some variants in content but not structure in his subsequent anthologies *Poemas (1935–1975)* (1979a) and *Obra poética I* (1997).[3] We must justify our definition of this phase in the psychological terms that we have laid out.

The key to this first phase, we believe, is a unitary process of personal development. We may speak of a period of introspective searching, of a desire for personal and poetic unity and integration, before Paz achieves the insights into history and time, and of the clarity of vision, which led to his classic masterpieces of the 1950s, *El laberinto de la soledad* and *Piedra de sol*. Surrealism, as we have said, opened the path for that search. In *Las peras del olmo*, Paz describes surrealism's deep attraction as follows: 'Surrealism – at its best and most valuable – will continue to be an invitation and a sign; an invitation to an internal adventure and the rediscovery of ourselves.'[4] Paz's guiding principle in this adventure, this voyage of discovery, was clarity. Conscious clarity, the 'lucidez' to which Jason Wilson aptly refers in his insightful examination of Paz and surrealism (1980, p. 35), sets Paz apart from the Freudian exercise of 'automatic writing' promoted by Breton.[5] Not only was it his guiding principle, but the very mark of his commitment to the poetic quest: as he states in the prologue to *Libertad bajo palabra*, 'esta lucidez ya no me abandona' (this lucidity will not abandon me).[6]

Clarity is the mark also of solitude: 'la soledad de la conciencia y la conciencia de la soledad.' The solitude of consciousness is described at length by Jung's disciple, Erich Neumann, in *The Origins and History of Consciousness* (1954; see especially s. A, pt 1, chap. 3). In the following pages, Neumann is an important voice that we integrate into our dialogue between Paz and Jung. Neumann defines solitude in emotional terms, using the word 'loneliness.' He speaks of the 'transition from the uroboros[7] to the adolescent stage' (p. 113) and of 'the feeling of loneliness, which is the necessary concomitant of egohood and particularly of an ego conscious of its own existence' (p. 115). In the first paragraph of *El laberinto de la soledad* Paz describes the consciousness of existence precisely as the adolescent stage:

> All of us, at some moment, have had a vision of our existence as something unique, untransferable and very precious. This revelation almost always takes place during adolescence. Self-discovery is above all the realization that we are alone: it is the opening of an impalpable, transparent wall – that of our consciousness – between the world and ourselves. It is true that we sense our aloneness almost as soon as we are born, but children and adults can transcend their solitude and forget themselves in games or work. The adolescent, however, vacillates between infancy and youth, halting for a moment before the infinite richness of the world. He is astonished at the fact of his being, and this astonishment leads to reflection: as he leans over the river of his consciousness, he asks himself if the face that appears there, disfigured by the water, is his own. The singularity of his being, which is pure sensation in children, becomes a problem and a question.[8] (1961, p. 9)

Despite the obvious mythical evocations of the image of the youth who sees his face reflected in the water of the river, this is not an image of narcissistic self-absorption and regression. The reflection in the water is the birth of that other, active reflection: reflection as reasoning and thought. Beyond his own image, the gaze of Paz's marvelling adolescent fills with the richness of the world. Most important, the content of the beginning of *El laberinto de la soledad* can be seen as a prelude, or at the very least an indication of the mindset which led to the poetic synthesis of *Piedra de sol.* Several important images which will later be developed in that poem are already present here in *El laberinto,* in an essential and dynamic interrelation: the river, the mirror, and the face.

This association between clarity and solitude does not negate the social dimension of Paz's surrealism and its utopian approach to the ideals of love, liberty, and the poetic imagination.[9] The social dimension of solitude is made clear at the end of *El laberinto*: solitude is the essential human condition and at the turning point of the twentieth century we find that 'Estamos al fin solos. Como todos los hombres' (p. 179; Finally we are alone. Like all mankind). Because, Paz argues, all of our grand systems of faith and reason have failed and we find ourselves alone with ourselves, we are for the first time contemporaries of all mankind: 'somos, por primera vez en nuestra historia, contemporáneos de todos los hombres' (p. 179). Solitude is then described by Paz, in the appendix to *El laberinto*, as a dialectic in which isolation and singularity are the very precondition of transcendence. Ceremony, celebration (*fiesta*), and ritual (above all, the verbal ritual of poetry) are the forms of communion by which that transcendence is achieved. Through them Man, a prisoner of linear, logocentric time, frees himself to emerge into living time (*tiempo vivo*), the spring (*manantial*) of the pure present, endlessly recreating itself (1959, p. 190). The spring is another important image, which will receive full expression in *Piedra de sol*.

The dialectic of communion is a continual process of creation, destruction, and recreation. Love, Paz states, contains both creation and destruction ('Creación y destrucción se funden en el acto amoroso'; 1959, p. 177). The poetic act, though, is a different form of transcendence because it is both communion and creative quest. To create his individual order out of chaos, the poet must possess clarity and lucidity of spirit because, as Paz states in *El arco y la lira*, 'Today poetry cannot be destruction of meaning but rather search for it. We know nothing of that meaning because the significance is not in what is said now but beyond, on a horizon that is scarcely perceptible' (1956b, 260). It is worthwhile quoting the same passage in the original Spanish because of the last phrase, 'aclara' (literally, 'is clarified'): 'Hoy la poesía no puede ser destrucción sino búsqueda del sentido. Nada sabemos de ese sentido porque la significación no está en lo que ahora se dice sino más allá, en un horizonte que apenas se aclara' (1956a, 282). The quest for clarity is the condition for poetic transcendence.

At first sight, Paz's search for conscious clarity and the criticism he expresses of Breton's 'sicologismo' and dependence on Freud (1971b, p. 132) would seem to be at odds with the 'aventura interior' of surrealism and with the approach that we adopt. Nevertheless, Paz's refusal to abandon active consciousness is not a negation of his introspective search, and we should not make the mistake of confusing introspection with introversion (understanding the latter term in its modern sense as coined, of course, by Jung). Paz, like the good extravert he is, seeks to carry out his introspective search through involvement and fusion with the object, the creation of a presence and dialogue with it.[10] This he attempts in the traditional mode of lyric poetical discourse: a first-person invocation of a poetic subject 'yo,' and evocation of a second person, referred to simply as 'tú.' Though all the poems that Paz writes during this period are personal, shorter works, without the epic traits of *Piedra de sol*, it would be a gross mistake to reduce the 'yo'–'tú' interchange to a dialogue between the poet and his beloved, as some have attempted to do. Though the 'tú' is in most (but not all) cases explicitly feminine[11] – and Paz, as we know, draws a specific parallel between poetic communion and erotic love – we should not forget that the 'yo' and the 'tú' often constitute the very structural axes of the poem itself and, as basic poles of meaning in a symbolic act, cannot be reduced to a single, particular meaning or *persona.*

As noted earlier, Paz's 'yo'–'tú' dialogue is a dialogue with the other: the other with the otherness of the opposite sex, external reality, creation, invented by the 'yo' and by which the 'yo' exists; and the other who is friend, accomplice, sister, brother, double, (s)he who invents the 'yo' but is also invented and given existence by the 'yo' in a reflexive, internal dialogue. As Paz expresses it in the prologue to *Libertad bajo palabra,* he 'invents' both the friend and fellow being who invents him, and woman, his opposite: 'Invento al amigo que me inventa, mi semejante; y a la mujer, mi contrario.' Perhaps because the poetic act in *Libertad bajo palabra* is precisely an introspective quest, because Paz is so totally immersed in the careful construction of the dialogue between self and other, he does not, at this stage, extend the image of friend and accomplice to the reader, the 'hypocrite lecteur, mon semblable, mon frère,' as Baudelaire describes him in *Les fleurs du mal.*

The other is the precondition for dialogue, but the dialogue of *Libertad bajo palabra* is intimate and incomplete, half-spoken in wonderment, sometimes fragmented in violence, half-heard. The constant thread, as we hope to demonstrate, is the introspective thrust of the poetry, which, as noted above, is not introversion but a desire to discover in and through the other the innermost and most deep-seated secrets of the self. Often we may speak of an invocation of and interchange with the 'tú,' rather than a dialogue. As Paz states in the prologue, there are no doors, only mirrors: 'Inútil tocar a puertas condenadas. No hay puertas, hay espejos. Inútil cerrar los ojos o volver entre los hombres: esta lucidez ya no me abandona. Romperé los espejos, haré trizas mi imagen que cada mañana rehace piadosamente mi cómplice, mi delator' (Useless to knock at condemned doors. There are no doors, only mirrors. Useless to close one's eyes or return to mankind: this lucidity will not abandon me. I will break the mirrors, smash my image into little pieces, and each morning my accomplice, my betrayer will piously reconstruct it).

As suggested here, the risk of the conscious ego being blinded by its own consciously constructed image is contained in the symbol of the mirror, which is a constant element in the poetry of this first stage, developing into the complex fullness with which it is expressed in *Piedra de sol.* Dialogue with the other and with the world is not, in this perspective, in any way an automatic or easy procedure. It is a privilege arduously fought for, and the introspective search is predicated on the constant necessity of the iconoclastic act. In Jungian terms, the ego must be prepared to constantly revision itself[12] to accede to the unconscious contents of the self. In this difficult process Paz fluctuates between dialogical and outright monological discourse, according to the inspiration behind each poem.

Commentary on the poems

At the most basic level, the invocation of the 'tú' is the establishment of a presence, as in the aptly titled 'Monólogo' from *Bajo tu clara sombra*:

Tu largo pelo rojizo
relámpago del verano,
vibra con dulce violencia
en la espalda de la noche.

Corriente oscura del sueño
que mana entre las ruinas
y te construye de nada. (SB:21; OP1:25)

(Your long red hair / flash of summer lightning, / trembles with sweet violence / on the back of night. / Dark dream current / springing among the ruins / shaping you from nothingness.)

And again, in the much later poem 'Cuerpo a la vista,' in *Semillas para un himno*:

Y las sombras se abrieron otra vez y mostraron un cuerpo:
tu pelo, otoño espeso, caída de agua solar,
tu boca y la blanca disciplina de sus dientes caníbales, prisioneros en llamas
tu piel de pan apenas dorado y tus ojos de azúcar quemada,
sitios en donde el tiempo no transcurre,
valles que sólo mis labios conocen,
desfiladero de la luna que asciende a tu garganta entre tus senos,
cascada petrificada de la nuca,
alta meseta de tu vientre,
playa sin fin de tu costado. (SB:126; OP1:116)

(And the shadows parted again to show a body: / your hair, thick autumn, fall of sun water, / your mouth and its white discipline of cannibal teeth, prisoners in flames / your skin of slightly toasted bread and your eyes of burnt sugar, / places where time does not pass, / valleys which only my lips know, / moon gorge which rises up to your throat between your breasts, / petrified cascade of the nape of your neck, / high plateau of your stomach, / endless beach of your side.)

The recurrent images throughout these poems are the woman's brilliant, falling hair and land forms rising from the sea as island, beach, and bay. These fundamental associations, which through their very recurrence suggest an unconscious origin, generate an extensive register of marine vocabulary in the second stanza of 'Atrás de la memoria' in *Puerta condenada*:

Bahías de hermosura, eternidades
substraídas, fluir vivo de imágenes,
delicias desatadas, pleamar,
(tu paladar: un cielo rojo, golfo
donde duermen tus dientes, caracola
donde oye la ola su caída) ... (SB:77; OP1:73)

(Bays of beauty, eternities / extracted, live flow of images / unleashed delights, high tide / (your palate: a red sky, a gulf / in which your teeth sleep, seashell / in which the wave hears its fall) ...)

For Jung the sea in dreams is the symbol par excellence of the collective unconscious. In the commentary on the third of the initial dreams in 'Individual dream symbolism in relation to alchemy'[13] he notes: 'The sea is the symbol of the collective unconscious, because unfathomed depths lie concealed beneath its reflecting surface. Those who stand behind, the shadowy personifications of the unconscious, have burst into the terra firma of consciousness like a flood' (1974, p. 122). The significance of Paz's comment, quoted above, that 'there are no doors, only mirrors' is here made clear: the reflecting surface of the sea does not allow the conscious ego to penetrate the depths beneath.

The sea is perhaps Paz's most frequent representation of the primeval liquid image of the unconscious, clearly associated with concave, sexual images of the feminine, whose relation to the archetypal and mythical image of hidden treasure and the realm of the sacred in the form of the communion host is made explicit in 'Cuerpo a la vista':

Entre tus piernas hay un pozo de agua dormida,
bahía donde el mar de noche se aquieta, negro caballo de espuma,
cueva al pie de la montaña que esconde un tesoro,
boca del horno donde se hacen las hostias,
sonrientes labios entreabiertos y atroces,
nupcias de la luz y la sombra, de lo visible y lo invisible
(allí espera la carne su resurrección y el día de la vida perdurable).

(SB:126–7; OP1:117)

(Between your legs lies a well of dormant water, / a bay where the night sea grows calm, black horse of foam, / a cave at the foot of the mountain which hides a treasure, / mouth of the oven where communion wafers are cooked, / smiling lips half-open and terrible, / wedding of light and shade, of the visible and the invisible / (there where flesh awaits its resurrection and the day of lasting life).)

The significance of the hidden treasure can also be illustrated from the thirteenth of Jung's initial dreams:

DREAM:
In the sea there lies a treasure. To reach it, he [the dreamer] has to dive through a narrow opening. This is dangerous, but down below he will find a companion. The dreamer takes the plunge into the dark and discovers a beautiful garden in the depths, symmetrically laid out, with a fountain in the centre.

The 'treasure hard to attain' lies hidden in the ocean of the unconscious, and only the brave can reach it. I conjecture that the treasure is also the 'companion,' the one who goes through life at our side – in all probability a close analogy to the lonely ego who finds a mate in the self, for at first the self is the strange non-ego. (1974, p. 191)

As Jung's commentary on the dream seeks to reveal, the other as counterpart ('contrario') is the door to the harmonious union of opposites, the synthesis of light and darkness, of what is visible and invisible to human consciousness. As companion and treasure, (s)he is both subject and object, contemplator and contemplated in the harmonious vision. This momentary synthesis or instant of comprehension and perception of harmony is what Paz seeks in the 'lightning flash,' as he describes it, of virtually every short poem in *Libertad bajo palabra.*

While rationalistic thought seeks to separate the continuity of the phenomenological world into abstract analytical components, symbolic thought looks to re-establish that continuity in associative harmonies of apparently disparate elements. A central task in this respect, whether in the tradition of religious thought, or philosophical or scientific enquiry before the eighteenth century, or modern poetry, is the union of paradoxical elements. In Paz, as we have noted, this is a constant enterprise, perceived with uncommon clarity; we find it from the very first phase of his texts as published in his collected poems. The most complete expression of this synthesis of paradox in this first phase is to be found in the series of six sonnets entitled simply 'Sonetos.' It is no mistake that for this purpose Paz chose the sonnet as the densest and most controlled of all traditional forms of versification in the western poetic tradition. The first of the series expresses the paradox of the static instant, the immobile climax of movement, the synthesis of rising and falling like the crest of a wave. The 'tú' represented here is a clear image of the anima, the archetypal projection of the female side of man, here identified with the motherly image of the 'spinning woman,' the dancer. Jung summarizes the projection as follows: 'The East calls it the "Spinning Woman" – Maya, who creates illusion by her dancing' (1959b, 11). Paz sees her as 'immobile in the light, but dancing':

Inmóvil en la luz, pero danzante,
tu movimiento a la quietud que cría
en la cima del vértigo se alía
deteniendo, no al vuelo, sí al instante.

Luz que no se derrama, ya diamante,
fija en la rotación del mediodía,
sol que no se consume ni se enfría
de cenizas y llama equidistante.

Tu salto es un segundo congelado
que ni apresura el tiempo ni lo mata:
preso en su movimiento ensimismado

tu cuerpo de sí mismo se desata
y cae y se dispersa tu blancura
y vuelves a ser agua y tierra obscura. (SB:22–3; OP1:26–7)

(Immobile in the light, but dancing, / your movement blends with the stillness it engenders / at the height of vertigo / freezing the moment, not the flight. /

Unpouring light, now diamond, / fixed in the rotation point of noon, / sun which neither burns nor cools / midway between ash and flame. /
Your leap is a frozen second / which neither hastens nor deadens time: / captive in its self-possessed movement. /
your body loosens from itself / and falls and your whiteness is dispersed / and you turn again to water and dark earth.)

There is a clear progression in this poem from the quatrains to the tercets: the 'tú' moves from original pure energy, movement, light to concrete form, but at the very moment of acquiring a body and entering time ('Tu salto ... tu cuerpo'), disperses into the elements of water and dark earth. Poetry seeks to enlighten for a moment psychical contents which inevitably shrink back into the dark unconscious.

Repetition and reflection are the key to the multiplicity of being of the 'tú' in the second sonnet:

El mar, el mar y tú, plural espejo,
el mar de torso perezoso y lento
nadando por el mar, del mar sediento:
el mar que muere y nace en un reflejo.

El mar y tú, su mar, el mar espejo:
roca que escala el mar con paso lento,
pilar de sal que abate el mar sediento,
sed y vaivén y apenas un reflejo.

De la suma de instantes en que creces,
del círculo de imágenes del año,
retengo un mes de espumas y de peces,

y bajo cielos líquidos de estaño
tu cuerpo que en la luz abre bahías
al obscuro oleaje de los días. (SB:23; OP1:27)

(The sea, the sea and you, plural mirror, / the slow and lazy torso of the sea / swimming in sea / thirsty for sea: / the sea which dies and is born in a reflection. /
The sea and you, its sea, the sea mirror: / rock with slow step climbing sea, / pillar of salt toppled by the thirsty sea, / thirst, and surge and ebb, and barely a reflection. /

From the sum of moments whence you grow, / from the ring of images of the year, / I retain a month of foam and fishes, /
And beneath steely liquid skies / your body opening bays of light / to the dark tide of days.)

This is one of the most subtle and complex of Paz's early poems. It presents paradox through an entirely different process than the first sonnet does. The constant repetition in the quatrains is a technique which attempts to break down a linear, rationalistic sequence and to liberate individual words to reflect subliminal associations. The unconscious sea and the 'tú,' the conscious construct, become a 'plural mirror,' reflecting each other back and forth. The mirror thus becomes both a metaphor for the poetic dialogue and the symbolic cornerstone of the poem's architecture. This architecture is based not on formal symmetries of the kind we found in the first sonnet, but on a moving symbolic process, a relation of meaning to meaning. Paul Ricoeur refers to such a relation as 'an architecture of meaning' in his explanation of the multiple meanings of the symbol: 'A symbol exists, I shall say, where linguistic expression lends itself by its double or multiple meanings to a work of interpretation. What gives rise to this work is an intentional structure which consists not in the relation of meaning to thing but in an architecture of meaning, in a relation of meaning to meaning, second meaning to first meaning, regardless of whether that relation be one of analogy or not, or whether the first meaning disguises the second meaning' (1970, 18).

The sea in its repetitions becomes both individualized persona and undifferentiated element, thereby permitting the paradox of being both the swimmer and the water she swims in. It is individualized through belonging ('su mar') and at the same time represents the sum total or the collective ('sumar'). The wordplay of 'su mar – sumar' and indeed various other aspects of this whole series of sonnets clearly have much in common with the surrealistic nocturnes of the *Contemporáneos* poet and playwright Xavier Villaurrutia, who at this stage, we should remember, is very much Paz's contemporary.[14] Yet there is also an earnestness of purpose in Paz's poem that foreshadows the techniques and philosophy of much later poems from *Blanco* on. This second sonnet may be seen as an incipient realization of the principle that language begets language, that poetic meaning arises not from the description of reality but from within words themselves.

The 'tú' of this second sonnet is again clearly associated with water images and the whiteness of the pillar of salt, which in archetypal terms are distinctly feminine. The 'tú' is a reflection of the sea, and the sea a reflection of the 'tú': the union of both is simultaneously the confirmation of the identity of the 'tú,' as illustrated by the subtle word play: 'sumar' (the sum total) is also 'su mar' (her sea). The view of the 'tú' as the 'sum of instants' presents the construction of the other as the very basis for the articulation of images which constitute the architecture of the poem. The body of the other is thus literally the body of the poem, the comfort of dry land ('bahías') wrested through mental energy ('luz') from the dark tides of unconsciousness and temporality. The tone changes radically in the tercets, where the carefully ordered syntactical structure and the orderly presentation of time in days, months, and the circle of the zodiac bear witness to the triumph of consciousness. Thus, the body of the poem is, in the final analysis, a careful construct, and it is therefore quite natural for Paz to have chosen the tight form of the sonnet in his pursuit of this goal.

In the third sonnet the same motif of repetition occurs but more indirectly, concealed perhaps in the baroque overtones of the syntax, with its inversions and the downright archaism of the 'porque' clause in the first quatrain:

> Del verdecido júbilo del cielo
> luces recobras que la luna pierde
> porque la luz de sí misma recuerde
> relámpagos y otoños en tu pelo. (SB:23; OP1:27)

> (From the greening joy of the sky / you glean bright lustre lost by moon / that light itself may thus recall / autumn lightning in your hair.)

Yet the decorative surface of the poem with its lively classical rhythm should not blind us to the deeper-lying, elemental source of that vitality. Nature is not simply the source of expressive images to describe the 'tú' (in a traditional sense, the image of the beloved). Nature *is* the 'tú,' the beloved. The feminine associations of water, and the whiteness of moon (quatrain 1) and ice (quatrain 2) clearly prolong the train of such images from previous sonnets (the pillar of salt in the second, for instance) and concern the archetypal, alchemical image of Luna. Luna, for the alchemists, was the cold, moist, feminine counterpart of Sol in the *coniunctio* or unification of opposite elements from which they sought to produce the philosopher's stone. In the course of this book, we shall have many occasions to return to these elements of the alchemical process, which Jung described and analysed in rich detail in studies collected in three major volumes of his collected works: *Psychology and Alchemy* (1944), *Alchemical Studies* (1968), and *Mysterium Coniunctionis* (1955–6).

Luna, in the sonnet in question, can also be seen as a reconfiguration of the mirror image (one of the meanings of the Spanish word *luna* being, precisely, 'mirror'): the moon reflects the light of the sun and the 'tú' reflects in her hair the light lost by the moon, thereby setting up the same 'plural mirror' we saw in the previous sonnet. What is new here is the association of the reflections with memory: the operative verb is 'recuerde.' The moon, the light, the 'tú' are distinctly personified and individualized as the objects of contemplation of the 'yo.' The 'tú' and associated images are mental projections of the 'yo' rather than his creative means as is true in the second sonnet.

The second quatrain introduces further archetypal images, notably the wind as symbol of spirit. In and of itself it moves in a circular fashion, swallowing its own tail, so to speak, but in a movement of descent into matter, it becomes a fertilizing image, as emphasized by the colour green, whose repetitions pervade the whole sonnet:

El viento bebe viento en su revuelo,
mueve las hojas y su lluvia verde
moja tus hombros, tus espaldas muerde
y te desnuda y quema y vuelve yelo.

Dos barcos de velamen desplegado
tus dos pechos. Tu espalda es un torrente.
Tu vientre es un jardín petrificado.

Es otoño en tu nuca: sol y bruma.
Bajo del verde cielo adolescente,
tu cuerpo da su enamorada suma. (SB:24; OP1:27–8)

(The wind drinks wind in its gusts, / moves the leaves and their green rain / dampens your shoulders, bites your back / strips and burns you, turns you to ice. /
Two boats with unfurled canvas / are your breasts. Your shoulder is a torrent. / Your belly is a garden turned to stone. /
The back of your neck glows in autumn rays and mists. / Under the green adolescent sky, / your body yields its lovestruck essence.)

The joyous associations of hope and growth afford no doubt sufficient motivation for the repeated use of the colour green here and a sufficient basis for its interpretation. The verbs of the second quatrain ('desnuda,' 'quema,' 'vuelve') hint, however, at a process of chemical transformation, which some reference to alchemy can elucidate for us. In *Mysterium Coniunctionis* Jung, in his extensive commentary on Abraham Eleazar's *Uraltes Chymisches Werck,* quotes the following declaration of the black Shulamite woman: 'But under my blackness I have hidden the fairest green'; he goes on to explain the colour in the following terms:

> It is the alchemical *benedicta viriditas,* the blessed greenness, signifying on the one hand the 'leprosy of the metals' (verdigris), but on the other the secret immanence of the divine spirit of life in all things. 'O blessed greenness, which generatest all things!' cries the author of the *Rosarium.* 'Did not the spirit of the Lord,' writes Mylius, Which is a fiery love, give to the waters when it was borne over them a certain fiery vigour, since nothing can be generated without heat? God breathed into created things ... a certain germination or greenness, by which all things should multiply ... They called all things green, for to be green means to grow ... Therefore this virtue of generation and the preservation of things might be called the Soul of the World.'

Green signifies hope and the future, and herein lies the reason for the Shulamite's hidden joy, which otherwise would be difficult to justify. But in alchemy green also means perfection. Thus, Arnaldus de Villanova says: 'Therefore Aristotle says in his book, Our gold, not the common gold, because the green which is in this substance signifies its total perfection, since by our magistery that green is quickly turned into truest gold' (Jung 1963, p. 432).

The various strands of symbolical and intertextual association explained here shed light on the process of the poem: the 'green rain' ('lluvia verde') is an agent of purification, reducing the feminine 'tú' to an elemental state of (lunar) whiteness ('yelo'). Yet the whiteness of the moon is also a reflection of the light of the sun, the 'fiery vigour' of spirit moving over the 'waters' of increate matter. The hair of the beloved reflects this light in the 'relámpagos y otoños en tu pelo,' an image which harks back to the Shulamite woman's depiction of her beloved in the biblical *Song of Songs,* which is also, of course, Eleazar's original point of reference: 'His head is as the most fine gold, his locks are bushy, and black as a raven' (chap. 5, v. 11). The reflection in Paz's poem, though, is conscious reflection: it is light 'remembering' itself, as the highly significant verb 'recuerde' shows. The suggestion of the archetypal content of the sonnet, then, is of a double process: the transformative 'greening' of nature, in which the 'tú' is or becomes a series of natural elements (ice, a waterfall, a petrified garden), and the process of conscious perfection, in which through 'magistery' the green is turned into purest, reflected gold. The 'magistery' in this case, we may assume, is that of the artist. The genesis of the other, we are beginning to see, happens at the intersection of nature and art as an interaction of spirit and matter, first as the emergence of living images into consciousness from the unconscious, then as the conscious moulding of these images into poetic structure. The 'tú' as the embodiment of such projections is, in the final analysis, an 'enamorada suma': a garden, a waterfall or fountain, a synthesis of sun and moon. The *Song of Songs* characterizes the beloved in much the same way:

> A garden inclosed is my sister, my spouse; a spring shut up, a fountain sealed. (chap. 4, v. 12)

> A fountain of gardens, a well of living waters, and streams from Lebanon. (chap. 4, v. 15)

> Who is she that looketh forth as the morning, fair as the moon, clear as the sun? (chap. 6, v. 10)

The fourth sonnet starts with what seems to be an allegorical depiction of a personified month of June. Underlying the name *June,* though, is an archetypal river of time, flowing from the past (this is the only one of the sonnets to use the past tense rather than the present).

> Bajo del cielo fiel Junio corría
> arrastrando en sus aguas dulces fechas,
> ardientes horas en la luz deshechas,
> frutos y labios que mi sed asía.
>
> Sobre mi juventud Junio corría:
> golpeaban mi ser sus aguas flechas,
> despeñadas y obscuras en las brechas
> que su avidez en ráfagas abría.

Ay, presuroso Junio nunca mío,
invisible entre puros resplandores,
mortales horas en terribles goces,

¡cómo alzabas mi ser, crecido río,
en júbilos sin voz, mudos clamores,
viva espada de luz entre dos voces! (SB:24; OP1:28)

(Under the sky ran faithful June / dragging dates in its fresh waters, / burning hours dissembled in the light, / fruits and lips seized by my thirst. /
Over my youthfulness ran June: / scourging my being with his arrows of water, / hurled down darkly in the clearings / opened in sudden blasts by his zeal. /
Oh, hasty June, never mine, / invisible amidst pure radiance, / mortal hours in terrible enjoyment, /
How you raised my being, swollen river, / in voiceless joyful chant, mute clamour, / living sword of light between two voices!)

The river is, for the fully conscious 'yo,' both a symbol of the impetuous flow of unconscious energy and desire and the dimension of his historical identity. The final tercet describes the emergence of voice: from the initial babblings raised from the unconscious ('júbilos sin voz, mudos clamores'), the river becomes the dividing 'sword of light between two voices.' The voices of the conscious and the unconscious? The voices of the 'yo' and the 'tú'? These are but different faces of the same reality, ultimately that of language: *voz* as voice and *voz* as word. The river is the living surge of light and the dividing sword of understanding.

The fifth sonnet returns to the paradoxical motif of the motionless movement in dance of the first sonnet, adding to this the paradox of presence and absence, or substance and insubstantiality ('la luz huidiza' and 'la playa no pisada'):

Cielo que gira y nube no asentada
sino en la danza de la luz huidiza,
cuerpos que brotan como la sonrisa
de la luz en la playa no pisada.

Qué fértil sed bajo tu luz gozada!
¡qué tierna voluntad de nube y brisa
en torbellino puro nos realiza
y mueve en danza nuestra sangre atada!

Vértigo inmóvil, avidez primera,
aire de amor que nos exalta y libra:
danzan los cuerpos su quietud ociosa,

danzan su propia muerte venidera,
arco de un solo son en el que vibra
nuestra anudada desnudez dichosa. (SB:25; OP1:28–9)

(Turning heaven, and cloud unfixed / save in the dance of fleeting light, / bodies that blossom like the smile / of light on an untrod beach.
Oh fertile thirst beneath your light enjoyed! / What tender will of cloud and breeze / sweeps us into purest swirl / and moves our captive blood in dance! /
Immobile frenzy, primal zeal, / air of love which frees, exalts us: / our bodies dance in leisured stillness, /
Dancing their approaching death, / arc of a single sound in which / our happy knot of nudity resounds.)

The amorous synthesis of opposites is achieved here, albeit in the brief instant of 'fleeting light,' the 'relámpago.' The embodied 'tú' and the embodied 'yo' are intertwined in 'nosotros,' and in the happy exaltation of erotic love ('de amor que nos exalta y libra'), a celebration of life which is also an announcement of, and preparation for, death.

This set of five sonnets can be seen as Paz's first clear demonstration of poetic genius and a prefiguration of the subject matter of *Piedra de sol.* Later, in 'La poesía' in 'Calamidades y milagros,' the 'tú' in the synthesis of opposites is poetry itself, and the 'yo' by implication is the poet. The poetic process is described in the same terms that we have explored in the sonnets:

Nublan mis ojos imágenes opuestas,
y a las mismas imágenes
otras, más profundas, las niegan,
ardiente balbuceo,
aguas que anega un agua más oculta y densa.
En su húmeda tiniebla vida y muerte,
quietud y movimiento, son lo mismo. (SB:105; OP1:98)

(Conflicting images cloud my sight, / and these same images / are cancelled out by other, deeper ones, / burning stutter, / waters drowned by a more hidden, thicker flood. / In its damp darkness life and death, / movement and stillness are the same.)

Yet the poet and poetry as personae for the 'yo'–'tú' dialogue underscore Paz's growing realization of the central importance of the word in the enunciation of poetic truth. While poetry is still a product of the unconscious self of the poet in the sense that

Subes desde lo más hondo de mí,
desde el centro innombrable de mi ser,
ejército, marea. (SB:104; OP1:97)

(You rise from my deepest depths, / from the unspeakable centre of my being, / army, tide.)

And it is his contact with the world:

Eres tan sólo un sueño,
pero en ti sueña el mundo
y su mudez habla con tus palabras. (SB:105; OP1:98)

(You are just a dream, / but the world dreams through you / and its silence speaks through your words.)

It is also an autonomous life force awakening tense pleasure and violent emotion:

Llegas, silenciosa, secreta,
y despiertas los furores, los goces,
y esta angustia
que enciende lo que toca. (SB:104; OP1:97)

(You come in silence and in secret, / and awaken passion, pleasure, / and this tense fear / which through touch enflames.)

The creation of a presence which has been the thrust of the 'yo'–'tú' dialogue up to now is here supplanted by a battle with a hostile, tyrannical 'tú' who inexorably subjugates the 'yo' to its will through thirst and desire:

Creces, tu sed me ahoga,
expulsando, tiránica,
aquello que no cede
a tu espada frenética. (SB:104; OP1:97)

(You grow, your thirst stifles me, / tyrannically expelling, / all that does not yield / to your frenzied sword.)

And the 'yo' must recognize his impotence:

Insiste, vencedora,
porque tan sólo existo porque existes,
y mi boca y mi lengua se formaron
para decir tan sólo tu existencia
y tus secretas sílabas, palabra
impalpable y despótica,
substancia de mi alma. (SB:105; OP1:98)

(Keep on, victorious one, / because only through your existence I exist, / and my mouth and tongue were formed / only to tell of your existence / and your secret syllables, unpalpable / despotic word, / substance of my soul.)

As the stanza makes plain, the very basis of the autonomy of the 'tú' as an adversary is language, the 'despotic word.' The 'tú,' now fully endowed with its own speech, not only the language of the world, is equipped to fulfil one of the essential functions of the anima figure, that of guide. Just as Beatrice did for Dante and Isis for Apuleius, so here Poetry will lead the poet. At least, this is the desire expressed in the final invocation of the poem:

Llévame, solitaria,
llévame entre los sueños,
llévame, madre mía,
despiértame del todo,
hazme soñar tu sueño,
unta mis ojos con tu aceite,
para que al conocerte me conozca. (SB:106; OP1:99)

(Carry me, solitary one, / carry me through your dreams, / carry me, mother mine, / awaken me fully, / make me dream your dream, / anoint my eyes with your oils, / so that in knowing you I know myself.)

As we can see from the vocatives used here ('solitaria' and 'madre mía'), there is still an essential connection between the archetype of the anima and that of the mother, the most primeval, plural, and undifferentiated of female images inhabiting the unconscious of both man and woman. Among the great variety of aspects and associations of the mother archetype mentioned by Jung (1959a, 81–4, the following will resonate as particularly pertinent: 'It [the mother archetype] can be attached to a rock, a cave, a tree, a spring, a deep well, or to various vessels ... or to vessel-shaped flowers like the rose or the lotus. Because of the protection it implies, the magic circle or mandala can be a form of mother archetype' (81). Like the youth staring into a well in wonderment at his own reflection in *The Labyrinth of Solitude* (*El laberinto de la soledad*), there is also still much of the adolescent in the poetic subject's expressions of rebellion, impotence, and final submission in this poem dedicated so explicitly to poetry as a persona.

In the poetry of the late 1940s and 1950s, *Semillas para un himno* and *¿Aguila o sol?*, the works where the imprint of surrealism is at its clearest, *the interior dialogue* gives way to a more objective idiom. While the 'tú' as a feminine presence embodying nature or in harmony with nature remains in uninterrupted continuity from the earlier poems, as we see in 'Cuerpo a la vista' (commented on earlier), 'Agua nocturna,' or 'Estrella interior,' she is more often objectified as 'mujer' or 'muchacha':

La mujer brilla como una alhaja ...
***
Reposa la mujer en la noche ... ('Estrella interior,' SB:147; OP1:134)

(The woman glistens like a jewel ... / The woman rests in night's repose ...)

Una mujer de movimentos de río
De transparentes ademanes de agua
Una muchacha de agua. ('Fábula,' SB:134; OP1:123)

(A woman moving like a river / With transparent water gestures / A girl of water.)

The structuring principle of the poem now appears to be not the dialogue but the evocative, metaphorical, even rhythmic potentialities of the individual word, as in this passage from 'Estrella interior':

Llorabas y reías
Palabras locas peces vivaces frutos rápidos

Abría la noche sus valles submarinos
En lo más alto de la hora brillaba el lecho con luz fija
En la más alta cresta de la noche brillabas
Atada a tu blancura
Como la ola antes que se derrame
Como la dicha al extender las alas
Reías y llorabas
Encallamos en arenas sin nadie
Muros inmensos como un No. (SB:148; OP1:135)

(You laughed and cried / Mad words lively fishes rapid fruits / The night opened its underwater valleys / At the summit of the hour the bed shone with a steady light / On the highest crest of the night you shone / Imprisoned in your whiteness / Like the wave before it falls / Like happiness as it spreads its wings / You laughed and cried / We ran aground on empty sands of silence / Walls as huge as a 'no.')

The arrangement of poems in stanzas gives way to long stretches which even have some of the qualities of medieval 'laisses' and are punctuated in paragraph form through repeated words, in this case 'reías' and 'llorabas.' In a way not seen in the earlier poetry, individual words seem to generate their own syntax as, for instance, in the second verse quoted above, where the nouns beget adjectives in a sequence without verbs, creating a break between verses one and three. At the same time as the repeated words create thematic centres around which the ensuing 'paragraphs' are organized, individual words are violating normal syntax in ways which break logical succession from verse to verse and liberate each verse as an entity in its own right. The construction of the poem is no longer driven by a symbolism of opposites but from within the word itself. All of the reasoning of the poem titled 'Semillas para un himno' revolves around the repetition of the words 'infrecuentes' and 'instantáneas,' and the process of poetic creation is described as follows:

Y brotaba instantánea imprevista la palabra convocada
        Pez
                Álamo
                        Colibrí
Y así ahora de mi frente zarpa un barco cargado de iniciales
Ávidas de encarnar en imágenes. (SB:151–2; OP1:138)

(And instanteously unforeseeably came forth the conjured word / Fish / Poplar / Hummingbird / And thus too now from my forehead a ship sails forth loaded with initials / Longing to take shape in images.)

Paz seems conscious, however, of the fragmentation of vision that each individual word's burden of logic implies. As he recounts in 'Fábula,' in the beginning there was a single word, which fragmented into the many words of our language with the birth of time:

Todos eran todo
Sólo había una palabra inmensa y sin revés
Palabra como un sol
Un día se rompió en fragmentos diminutos
Son las palabras del lenguaje que hablamos
Fragmentos que nunca se unirán
Espejos rotos donde el mundo se mira destrozado. (SB:134; OP1:123)

(Each of them was the one and only / There was only one huge one-sided word / A word like a sun / One day it broke into tiny fragments / Which are the words of the language we speak / Fragments which will never be united / Broken mirrors for the world to see its shattered self.)

To rise above this fragmentation, to achieve communion, is the battle of the poet with poetry, and the struggle begins with the word, an arduous circular struggle beginning over and over again, a game of chance, as the poet describes it in his prefatory remarks in *¿Aguila o sol?*: 'Hoy lucho a solas con una palabra. La que me pertenece, a la que pertenezco: ¿cara o cruz, águila o sol?' (SB:163; OP1:145; Today I struggle alone with a word. The one belonging to me, to which I belong: heads or tails, eagle or sun?)

At this point in his career, Paz's introspective search leads him fairly and squarely towards the theory of poetic creation. While *¿Aguila o sol?* may be in some respects an adventure in poetic prose, it is also an attempt to mix genres, his first attempt to bring poetic form closer to that of the essay. There is a clear and ordered progression from one part of the work to another, leading to the culminating high point 'Hacia el poema.' As the subtitle 'Puntos de partida' suggests, this is not an end, but rather a beginning. The struggle of the poet ends where the poem begins; the present ends where the future begins. The approximation of poetry to essayistic form may be motivated, here, by a desire to underline the moral dimension of the poetic message, to confer a tone of poetic manifesto to 'Hacia el poema' with its famous last line: 'Merece lo que sueñas': 'Deserve what you dream.' Yet the form is still fragmentary. On the surface, 'Hacia el poema' has a hymn- or psalm-like structure, apparently divided into extensive biblical-style verses, reminiscent of the poetry of Walt Whitman. A closer reading will reveal that these 'verses' are a set of proto-poems with intercalary thoughts, undeveloped starting points of words and images which express a Utopian confidence in a new beginning of understanding and freedom:

> Por todas partes los solitarios forzados empiezan a crear las palabras del nuevo diálogo.
>
> El poema prepara un orden amoroso. Preveo un hombre-sol y una mujer-luna, el uno libre de su poder, la otra libre de su esclavitud, y amores implacables rayando el espacio negro. Todo ha de ceder a esas águilas incandescentes.
>
> Mediodía futuro, árbol inmenso de follaje invisible. En las plazas cantan los hombres y las mujeres el canto solar, surtidor de transparencias. Me cubre la marejada amarilla: nada mío ha de hablar por mi boca. (SB:229; OP1:194)
>
> (Everywhere those living in obligatory solitude are beginning to create the words of the new dialogue. / The poem prepares a realm of love. I foresee a sun-man and a moon-woman, the former free from his power, the latter free from her slavery, and implacable gestures of love streaking across black space. Everything must give way to these incandescent eagles. / Midday of the future, vast tree of invisible foliage. In the town squares men and women sing the solar song, fountain of transparencies. I am covered by the golden flood: nothing merely mine shall be spoken by my lips.)

The last line of the last segment quoted, 'nada mío ha de hablar por mi boca,' reflects Paz's realization that the poetic act, born from personal introspection can be poetic only in a social and collective sense. Words expressed by 'solitarios' are just that: words. Poetry begins when the poet communes with his reader or listener and both are transported into another realm, projected onto 'the other shore' through a 'mortal leap,' as Paz outlines in a terminology borrowed from the *sutras.* The dimension that has been added since the early poetry and seems to motivate this realization of the social and moral importance of poetry as act, is the sense of History:[15]

Cuando la Historia duerme, habla en sueños: en la frente del pueblo dormido el poema es una constelación de sangre. Cuando la Historia despierta, la imagen se hace acto, acontece el poema: la poesía entra en acción.

('Hacia el poema,' SB:230; OP1:194)

(When History sleeps, it speaks in dreams: in the forehead of the sleeping people the poem is a constellation of blood. When History awakens, the image becomes act, the poem happens: poetry is set in motion.)

The various conceptual dimensions of *¿Aguila o sol?* lead in different directions to the genesis of Paz's three key works of the 1950s: the sense of History leads to the writing of *El laberinto de la soledad*, the sense of the mission of poetry leads to the theory of poetic creation and transcendence ('la otra orilla') in *El arco y la lira*, and the poem to which the fragments of 'Hacia el poema' point is *Piedra de sol*.

The final section of *Libertad bajo palabra*, 'La estación violenta,' is an exploration of History. Each of this series of relatively long poems, culminating in the longest of all, *Piedra de sol*, bears a specific place-time connection: Naples 1948, Venice 1948, Avignon 1949, Paris 1950, Delhi 1952, and so on, culminating in the poet's return to his place of origin, Mexico, with 'El cántaro roto' (1955) and *Piedra de sol* (1957). The 'yo'–'tú' dialogue has completely disappeared at this stage, and the poet is in a new dialogue with History, with the objective world. The essence of this dialogue is a questioning which comes to the fore in explicit fashion, for instance, in '¿No hay salida?' The past is a set of broken images, a city in ruins, inhabited by the dead. Jung would remind us here that the city and the world of the dead are manifestations of the negative side of the mother archetype (1959a, 81–2). And Paz, in turn, would remind us of one of the 'puntos de partida' (points of departure) of 'Hacia el poema': 'Cortar el cordon umbilical, matar bien a la Madre' (SB:228; OP1:193; 'Cut the umbilical cord, completely kill the Mother'). Many of the architectural images of the poems concern this almost obsessive broken city of the dead leitmotif:

¡Estatua rota,
columnas comidas por la luz,
ruinas vivas en un mundo de muertos en vida!

('Himno entre ruinas,' SB:233; OP1:195)

(Broken statue, / columns corroded by the light, / living ruins in a world of living dead!)

he aquí a la piedra rota, al hombre roto, a la luz rota.
('El cántaro roto,' SB:257; OP1:215)

(behold the broken stone, broken man, broken light.)

For the individual conscious of his solitude, now separated from the mother and the comfort of pre-established order and primeval significance, the challenge is to take responsibility for creating his own meaning in an otherwise senseless world and existence:

el desprendido de su madre, el desterrado, el sin raíces, ni cielo ni tierra, sino puente, arco
tendido sobre la nada, en sí mismo anudado, hecho haz, y no obstante partido en dos desde el nacer, peleando
contra su sombra, corriendo siempre tras de sí, disparado, exhalado, sin jamás alcanzarse,
el condenado desde niño, destilador del tiempo, rey de sí mismo, hijo de sus obras. ('Mutra,' SB:247; OP1:207)

(he who is separated from his mother, the exiled one, with no roots, nor heaven nor earth, but a bridge, an arch / stretched over nothing, bound up within himself, tied as a sheaf, and yet split into two from birth, struggling / with his shadow, always running after himself, shot forth, exhaled, never catching up with himself, / the one condemned from birth, steeped in time, king over himself, child of his own deeds.)

The question is how to synthesize these broken and, in principle, meaningless, fragments into a unity of presence, of the present of the 'yo,' not as an isolated but as a collective being, as mankind itself:

¿Dónde está el hombre, el que da vida a las piedras de los muertos, el que hace hablar piedras y muertos? ('Mutra,' SB:246; OP1:206)

(Where is Man, he who gives life to the stones of the dead, he who makes stones and the dead to speak?)

Though in his classic study on *La estación violenta* Carlos Magis observes that few critics initially saw that the purpose of its surrealist language was to 'alzar la palabra y no para levantar laberintos' (1978, p. 201), it is clear from the passages quoted above from 'Mutra' that there is something labyrinthine in the individual's quest: he must constantly 'fight against his shadow,' 'run after himself without ever catching up'; he is 'condemned since childhood' to struggle, yet is 'king with dominion over his being.' The same labyrinthine sense is present in each of the poems and in their very succession. The 'yo' is conscious of the circularity of his quest, of returning to the point of origin:

> todo se ha cerrado sobre sí mismo, he vuelto a donde empecé, todo es hoy y para siempre. ('¿No hay salida?' SB:250; OP1:209)

> (everything has closed in upon itself, I am back where I started, everything is today and forever)

And of the challenge of exploring pathways where the clear light of reason cannot penetrate:

> galerías que recorro con los ojos vendados. ('El río,' SB:252; OP1:210)

> (galleries through which I move blindfold.)

In the mid-point of the labyrinth there is a strong sense of abandonment and isolation:

> A mitad del poema me sobrecoge siempre un gran desamparo, todo me abandona,
>
> no hay nadie a mi lado, ni siquiera esos ojos que desde atrás contemplan lo que escribo,
> no hay atrás ni adelante, la pluma se rebela, no hay comienzo ni fin ...
> ('El río,' SB:253; OP1:211)

> (At the midpoint of the poem I am always overcome by a huge sense of helplessness, I am left all alone, there is no one by my side, not even those eyes behind me observing what I write / there is no one in front of me or behind, my pen rebels, there is no end or beginning ...)

Yet underneath the multiple images of the labyrinth a number of recurring archetypal images signal a way forward and constitute the very energy of the poem. They surge up from the unconscious like water from a subterranean fountain. We may identify the following images:

the stone (often envisaged as a symbol of the self),[16] the river (which for Paz is of ink and of blood, the written word and existence itself, associated with the sea, image of the unconscious), the fountain (from which springs the sacred 'living water' of renewal, an image also associated with the tree), the city (symbol on many occasions of both the mother and the anima archetypes), and the king (the hero). All these images speak clearly of the process of rebirth and individuation, as explained in Jung's most widely known works, the essays contained in *The Archetypes and the Collective Unconscious* (1959a) and the book *Aion* (1959b).

To take each of the symbols mentioned in turn: in 'Mutra' the stone is seen as a centre endowed with life and spirit (a 'zócalo del relámpago'), a time-bound, yet time-resistant, monument:

> No, asir la antigua imagen: ¡anclar el ser y en la roca plantarlo, zócalo del relámpago!
> Hay piedras que no ceden, piedras hechas de tiempo, tiempo de piedra, siglos que son columnas,
> asambleas que cantan himnos de piedra,
> surtidores de jade, jardines de obsidiana, torres de mármol, alta belleza armada contra el tiempo. (SB:246; OP1:206)

> (No, to grasp the ancient image: anchor being and plant it in the rock, plinth of lightning! / There are stones that do not yield, stones made of time, time of stone, centuries which are pillars, / gatherings singing hymns of stone, / jade fountains, gardens of obsidian, ivory towers, tall beauty armed against time.)

The vital association of stones (the plural is significant) with human beings and their history, as well as the specifically Mexican references, are evident in this passage. We can trace a direct continuity between these references and the Aztec calendar or sun stone of *Piedra de sol.* The reference to 'surtidores de jade' is especially interesting, since here the stone is of a precious kind (jade), is green in colour, and is associated with the fountain. We may compare such a reference to the biblical rock, which when struck produces living water, and the association of both symbols in Christ.

The river is one of the most pervasive and recurrent images in the poems of *La estación violenta.* Its symbolism is quite simple as a figure of the unconscious, and of time. It traces the flow of the history of mankind from its origins:

como un solo río interminable bajo arcos de siglos fluyen las estaciones y los hombres,
hacia allá, al centro vivo del origen, más allá de fin y comienzo.
('El cántaro roto,' SB:258; OP1:216)

(as a single unending river under the arches of the centuries flow seasons and men, / to the beyond, the living centre of origin, beyond all end and all beginning.)

In the poem entitled 'El río,' it is described as both a 'río de sangre' (the blood of existence) and a 'río de tinta' (the ink of words and language), but it is ancient, collective, undifferentiated existence and pre-language, the primeval state existing before the birth of the individual consciousness:

discurso incomprensible y jadeante, un tartamudeo de aguas y piedra batallando, su historia ...
sílabas de tiempo, letras rotas, gotas de tinta, sangre que va y viene y no dice nada y me lleva consigo. ('El rio,' SB:252–3; OP1:211–2)

(incoherent, gasping discourse, stutter of battling waters and stone, its story ... / syllables of time, broken letters, drops of ink, blood which ebbs and flows and says nothing and carries me with it.)

Its flow also represents the battle for the birth of language:

toda la noche las piedras rotas se buscan a tientas en mi frente, toda la noche pelea el agua contra la piedra,
las palabras contra la noche, la noche contra la noche, nada ilumina el opaco combate. ('El rio,' SB:254; OP1:212)

(all night long the broken stones grope for each other in my forehead, all night long water battles with stone, / words with the night, night with the night, no light shines through the dense dark combat)

It is the primeval Word which exists before the birth of words, and it is associated with sleep and with night:

borrar mi imagen de río que habla dormido y no dice nada y me lleva consigo
...

el incendio y la destrucción y el nacimiento del instante y la respiración de la noche fluyendo enorme a la orilla del tiempo.
decir lo que dice el río, larga palabra semejante a labios, larga palabra que no acaba nunca. ('El rio,' SB:252–3; OP1:211)

(efface my image of a river speaking in sleep, saying nothing and carrying me with it ... / the fire and the destruction and the birth of the moment and the breath of the night flowing vast along the banks of time. / to tell what the river says, a long word like a pair of lips, a long and never-ending word.)

And with the archetype par excellence of the unconscious, the sea:

decir lo que dice el tiempo en duras frases de piedra, en vastos ademanes de mar cubriendo mundos. ('El rio,' SB:253; OP1:212)

(to tell what time says in hard sentences of stone, in giant gestures of sea covering worlds.)

The king or hero archetype is much more diffusely represented in these poems, perhaps because Man as protagonist is seen as an uprooted, dispossessed, post-Edenic figure, an inheritor of broken images, from which he can wrest, initially, only an individual sense:

Y el hombre es hombre, el que saltó al vacío y nada lo sustenta desde entonces sino su propio vuelo.
el desprendido de su madre, el desterrado, el sin raíces, ni cielo ni tierra, sino puente, arco
tendido sobre la nada, en sí mismo anudado, hecho haz, y no obstante partido en dos desde el nacer, peleando
contra su sombra, corriendo siempre tras de sí, disparado, exhalado, sin jamás alcanzarse,
el condenado desde niño, destilador del tiempo, rey de sí mismo, hijo de sus obras. ('Mutra,' SB:247; OP1:207)

(And Man is man, he who leapt into the void and is henceforth borne only on the wings of his own flight. / he who is separated from his mother, the exiled one, with no roots, nor heaven nor earth, but a bridge, an arch / stretched over nothingness, bound up within himself, tied as a sheaf, and yet split into two from birth, struggling / with his shadow, always running after himself, shot forth, exhaled, never catching up with himself, / the one condemned from birth, steeped in time, king over himself, child of his own deeds.)

As the last verse indicates, he is king only over himself.

Nevertheless, many of the traditional motifs associated with the King archetype occur in the description of the new day at the beginning of 'Mutra,' such as the regal lion and lioness, the sun, the throne, the fiery nature of sulphur:[17]

Como una madre demasiado amorosa, una madre terrible que ahoga,
como una leona taciturna y solar,
como una sola ola del tamaño del mar,
ha llegado sin hacer ruido y en cada uno de nosotros se asienta como un rey
y los días de vidrio se derriten y en cada pecho erige un trono de espinas y de brasas. (SB:244; OP1:204)

(Like an over-zealous mother, a terrible stifling mother, / like a silent solar lioness, / like a single wave the size of the sea, / it has noiselessly arrived and in each of us sets up throne like a king / and the days of glass melt away and in each breast it establishes its throne of thorns and coals.)

The classic process of dismemberment of the King as a prelude to rebirth, so familiar in legend and explored at length by Jung in various of his writings,[18] seems at first condemned to abortive failure:

he aquí al polvo que se levanta como un rey amarillo y todo lo descuaja y danza solitario y se derrumba
como un árbol al que de pronto se le han secado las raíces, como una torre que cae de un solo tajo,
he aquí al hombre que cae y se levanta y como polvo se arrastra,
el insecto humano que perfora la piedra y perfora los siglos y carcome la luz,
he aquí a la piedra rota, al hombre roto, a la luz rota.
('El cántaro roto,' SB:257; OP1:215)

(behold the dust arising like a yellow king dissolving everything in his solitary dance, then falling / like a tree whose roots have suddenly withered, like a tower felled with a single slash, / behold man falling, rising again, dragging along the ground like dust, / the human insect boring through stone and boring through the centuries and eating away at light, / behold the broken stone, broken man, broken light.)

Finally, though, it is in his persona as poet, through his collective mission of speaking for all of humankind, that the sacrifice of the individual as hero will triumph:

> En el centro de la plaza la rota cabeza del poeta es una fuente.
> La fuente canta para todos. ('Fuente,' SB:241; OP1:202)

> (In the centre of the square the broken head of the poet is a fountain / The fountain sings for all.)

The fountain is the most complex of the archetypal symbols mentioned, by virtue of its associations with stone and tree and the royal couple (*Rex* and *Regina*, King and Queen) of alchemy. Jung elucidates the associations in a commentary on a parable related by Bernardus Trevisanus: 'He tells the parable of an adept who finds a clear spring set about with the finest stone, and "secured to the trunk of an oak-tree," the whole surrounded by a wall. This is the King's bath in which he seeks renewal. An old man, Hermes, the mystagogue, explains how the King had this bath built: he placed in it an old oak, "cloven in the midst." The fountain was surrounded by a thick wall, and "first it was enclosed in hard, bright stone, then in a hollow oak"' (1963, p. 70). Jung goes on to note:

> The point of the parable, evidently, is to bring the oak into connection with the bath. Usually this is the nuptial bath of the royal pair. But here the Queen is missing, for it is only the King who is renewed. This unusual version of the motif suggests that the oak, as the feminine numen, has taken the place of the Queen. If this assumption is correct, it is particularly significant that the oak is said to be 'cloven' and later to be 'hollow.' Now it seems to be the upright trunk or 'stock' of the fountain, now a living tree casting a shadow, now the trough of the fountain. This ambiguity refers to the different aspects of the tree: as the 'stock,' the oak is the source of the fountain, so to speak; as the trough it is the vessel, and as the protecting tree it is the mother. (pp. 70–1)

The tree is also associated with the anima figure, the male's unconscious projection of his feminine side: 'Often, as in the Ripley Scrowle, the tree stands in the nuptial bath, either as a pillar or directly as a tree in whose branches the numen appears in the shape of a mermaid (= anima) with a snake's tail' (p. 71). In other words, the parable quoted by Jung above is an allegory not of nuptial union, the *coniunctio*, but of rebirth, in which the self is born and defines itself in relation to a primeval, undifferentiated image of femininity: the archetype of the Great Mother. The tree is mother, spouse, and anima. For the King (the hero, the protagonist) the female symbolizes both origin and quest and union.

The archetypal significance of the close association of fountain and tree, which we will see in *Piedra de sol*, now becomes apparent. Woman in that poem is the goddess Coatlicue (Earth Mother), as well as muse, or anima, and lover. In a real sense, the poem 'Fuente' in *La estación violenta* (dated 1949 in Avignon) is a prelude to *Piedra de sol* in its exploration of the significance of the symbol and the rebirth process in its collective, historical sense, exploiting the double meaning of *fuente* in Spanish as both 'fountain' or 'spring' (*manantial*) and 'source, origin.' The 'fuente' here is a dynamic centre of movement in which liquid light, emerging from the old stones of the past, reaches up to the sky and pours out into the present:

> El viejo mundo de las piedras se levanta y vuela.
> Es un pueblo de ballenas y delfines que retozan en pleno cielo, arrojándose grandes chorros de gloria;
> y los cuerpos de piedra, arrastrados por el lento huracán de calor,
> escurren luz y entre las nubes relucen, gozosos. (SB:239; OP1:200)

> (The old world of stones rises up and takes flight. / It is a populace of whales and dolphins romping through the open sky, shooting great jets of glory over one another; / and the stone bodies, dragged by the slow hurricane of heat, ooze light and shine joyfully among the clouds.)

The image of the city (mentioned above as associated with the mother and anima archetypes) is invoked as the central symbol of this process of liberation from time and the past, pouring itself, emptying itself into the present. This is clearly the liberation of the anima as a separate and distinct presence:

> La ciudad lanza sus cadenas al río y vacía de sí misma,
> de su carga de sangre, de su carga de tiempo, reposa
> hecha un ascua, hecha un sol en el centro del torbellino.
> El presente la mece. (SB:239; OP1:200)

> (The city casts its chains into the river and emptied of itself, / of its load of blood, of its load of time, takes rest, / having become a burning coal, a sun in the middle of the whirlwind. / It is cradled by the present.)

In so doing, it (she) becomes fire, sun, a masculine presence, in a process of masculinization underlined grammatically by the passage from an overtly marked feminine noun through the gender-neutral article *UN* to the masculine noun *sol*: 'LA ciudad [*feminine*] ... hecha UN [*neutralization of feminine/masculine*] ascua [*feminine*], hecha UN sol [*masculine*].' The ambiguity of this process is clear, though, from the later contrary image of the city, not as changing into sun, but holding the sun in the hollow of her hand. At this point, it/she clearly is associated with liquid images, the jets of the fountains:

La ciudad sigue en pie.
Tiembla en la luz, hermosa.
Se posa el sol en su diestra pacífica.
Son más altos, más blancos, los chorros de las fuentes. (SB:240; OP1:201)

(The city still stands. / It trembles, beautiful, in the light. / The sun alights upon its calm right hand. / The jets of the fountains are taller, whiter.)

The same association also recurs in other poems of the series, as, for example, in 'Mutra': 'la muchacha que aparece en la plaza y es un chorro de frescura pausada' (SB:244; OP1:205; the girl who appears in the square and is a slow, cool jet of water), and the symbolism of the transformative process is elucidated towards the end of 'El cántaro roto':

el agua de la mujer, el manantial para beber y mirarse y reconocerse y recobrarse,
el manantial para saberse hombre, el agua que habla a solas en la noche y nos llama con nuestro nombre,
el manantial de las palabras para decir yo, tú, él, nosotros, bajo el gran árbol viviente estatua de lluvia ... (SB:258; OP1:216)

(the water of woman, the spring in which to drink and see oneself and recognize oneself and recover oneself, the spring in which man knows he is a man, the water speaking alone in the night and calling us by name, / the spring of words to say I, you, he, we, under the great tree living statue of rain)

Water is female, as spring and origin, but is the very element of the birth (and rebirth) of masculine identity, for which process it becomes, interestingly enough, a fountain of language. The spring (anima) rises under the shadow of the great tree (mother archetype).

At the end of 'Fuente,' the dual, contradictory nature of the fountain, rising and falling, dark and light, is emphasized:

Todo se pone en pie para caer mejor ...
la columna transparente que un instante se obscurece y otro centellea,
según avanza la veloz escritura del destino. (SB:240–1; OP1:201–2)

(Everything rises up the better to fall ... / the transparent pillar alternately glowing and fading, / as dictated by the rapid hand of destiny.)

The final verses of the poem, however, describe the synthesis between the city and the poet, the feminine and the masculine, between matter, on the one hand, and mind or spirit on the other:

En el centro de la plaza la rota cabeza del poeta es una fuente.
La fuente canta para todos. (SB:241; OP1:202)

(In the centre of the square the broken head of the poet is a fountain. / The fountain sings for all.)

The synthesis derives from the collective mission of the poet: the fountain sings for all. In *Piedra de sol* this both traditional and surrealist image of the fountain of poetry and inspiration becomes richer and more complex through associations with time, the self, and existence in general. Nevertheless, the collective sense and the desire for the 'encuentro' (harmonious synthesis) remain the same.

'El cántaro roto,' which, as we indicated above, is the return to Mexico from the geographical itinerary represented in the other poems of *La estación violenta,* is a summing up, a clarification of the function of this series of poems as a whole and as a prelude to *Piedra de sol.* What is new, however, in *Piedra de sol* is the association of the symbols of fountain and river in a single geometrical (vertical-horizontal) construct.[19] The unconscious river rises into consciousness through the fountain. The symbol of the mirror now assumes a central importance: the fountain mirrors the circular form of the river, just as the individual conscious ego takes form in the unconscious collective mirror of the self. The 'I,' like Quetzalcoatl in the Aztec legend holding the mirror given to him by his adversary Tezcatlipoca, looks into it and sees that he has a face.[20] In so doing he discovers his own mortality, that he has a destiny, that he is an individual who is subject to History. The 'I'–'you' dialogue with its varied transformations and diverse avatars has run its course. We are ready for a new stage of synthesis.

Phase Two

Piedra de sol: The Birth of Ego Consciousness and the Search for Self

Introduction

Before we begin our commentary on *Piedra de sol* and the Jungian symbols and concepts which can illuminate its meaning, it is useful to briefly examine some prefatory materials relating to the ideas of history, cosmogony, and time with which Paz was preoccupied at the beginning of this second phase of his creative development, during which he emerged as a world-famous, internationally recognized poet. We hope that the reader will bear with us in our attention to prefatory detail, knowing that it relates to Paz's essential purpose in this, his first long poem.

In a televised presentation on pre-Columbian art,[1] Paz describes Meso-American history in the following terms:

> The history of Meso-America can be seen not only as a succession of events ... but also as an enormous dramatic ritual ceremony. That is why it draws us with passion and fascinates us. The theme of this ceremony, repeated over and over in every culture and epoch, is the myth of genesis, the creation of the world, the destruction of the world. Creation – destruction, creation – destruction, this is the idea at the centre of Meso-American civilization. Not the linear succession of western history, but rather, a mythical vision of human events. History repeats itself, as do the days and the years, eras and centuries, the planets and the constellations. The history of humankind is an episode in the history of heavenly bodies and cosmologies.[2]

This is the perspective which informs Paz's intellectual self-questioning at the end of the 1950s and engenders his two most universally known works: his personal disquisition on Mexican culture and history, *El laber-*

into de la soledad, and his poetic synthesis of personal, generational, national and universal history in *Piedra de Sol.* The title refers to the famous Aztec calendar stone or sun stone, a large circular representation of the Mexican creation myth of the five suns, carved in stone during the reign of the last Aztec king, Motecuhzoma II Xocoyotzin, and currently located in the Mexican National Museum of Anthropology. The stone bears in its centre the face of the sun god, Tonatiuh, who is surrounded by the emblems of four previous 'suns' or creations of the world, creating thereby a sum of five cardinal points (north, south, east, west, and centre), around which the circular structure of the stone is organized. These are in turn encircled by glyphs of the twenty days of the Aztec month. The sun's rays point towards the outermost circle, formed by two descending serpents, representing time and the universe itself. Two faces appearing from the jaws of the serpents are the Mexican deities Quetzalcoatl, as the face of sun and light, and Tezcatlipoca in his manifestation as Xiuhtecutli, god of night and darkness. They are, as Leticia Underwood notes, 'joined by their tongues to symbolize the continuity of time' (1992, 70).

This synthesis of duality or union of opposites represented in the sun stone points to the intertwining of the creation myth with other myths, particularly that of Quetzalcoatl, who as both god and virtuous ruler-priest is shown a reflection of his own mortality in a mirror by his arch-enemy Tezcatlipoca, becomes corrupted through drink and incestual carnal knowledge, and is sacrificed on a pyre, whence a star (Venus) is born. Quetzalcoatl descends into the netherworld of Mictlan, from where he emerges and ascends into the firmament, carrying with him the bones of the ancient dead, restored to life. This association of death and rebirth with the creation myth is quite natural in the Mexican cosmogony, which establishes a direct and natural relation between the individual and the universe. The individual's birth is seen as a descent from the womb of the great Earth Mother into time and mortality, and his/her possibility of redemption or regeneration depends almost entirely on the interlocking influences of the astral bodies. This universal, fatalistic view is the backdrop of reference in *Piedra de sol.* We should remember that it is quite different from the Christian view of death and rebirth, centred upon the individual's identification with the person of Christ through the sacrament of baptism.

Piedra de sol stands out, not only as the first of a series of longer poems marking moments of synthesis in Paz's poetic production, but also as a watershed for his critics. It is with *Piedra de sol* that Paz first establishes a truly international reputation as Mexico's foremost national poet. Critics in both Mexico and the United States have explored in detail the references to Mexican indigenous mythology and cosmogony on which the circular structure of the poem is based. Such explorations follow naturally from the reference to the Aztec sun stone described above as well as from Paz's own prefatory note to the first edition of the poem, which runs as follows:

> On the cover of this book the number 585 appears in the Mayan writing system, and the Mexican signs for the days 4 Ollin (Movement) and 4 Ehécatl (Wind) are included at the beginning and end of the poem. It is perhaps not inappropriate to mention that this poem is composed of 584 hendecasyllables (the last six do not count because they are the same as the first six, and in fact the poem does not end with them but rather begins again). This number of verses is equal to the 584 days of the synodical revolution of the planet Venus. The ancient Mexicans counted the cycle of Venus (and that of other planets visible to the naked eye) from the day 4 Ollin; the day 4 Ehécatl marked a point 584 days after the conjunction of Venus and the Sun and therefore the end of a cycle and the beginning of a new one. The interested reader will find more complete (and better) information on this matter in the studies devoted to the topic by Raúl Noriega, to whom I am indebted for this data.
>
> The planet Venus is visible twice a day as the Morning Star (Phosphorus) and Evening Star (Hesperus). This duality (Lucifer and Vesper) has never ceased to impress men from all civilizations, who have seen in it a symbol, a cipher or embodiment of the essential ambiguity of the universe. Thus it is that Ehécatl, god of the wind, was one of the incarnations of Quetzalcoatl, the plumed serpent, who represents the double-sided nature of life. In its associations with the Moon, dampness, water, new vegetation, and the death and resurrection of nature, the planet Venus was for the ancient peoples of the Mediterranean a hub of ambivalent forces and images: Istar, the Lady of the Sun, the Conical Stone, the Unsculpted Stone (reminiscent of Taoism's 'piece of unpolished wood'), Aphrodite, Cicero's fourfold Venus, Pausanias' dual goddess etc.[3]

Apart from the explanation of the precise length and the circular nature of the poem, what strikes one in Paz's note is the detailed attention given to Venus, which goes well beyond the immediate association with the man-god Quetzalcoatl, to include Mediterranean and even oriental references. Another interesting fact concerning this note is its omission in subsequent editions, although, as Underwood points out, it reappears in abbreviated form in the bilingual edition of his poetry: *The Collected Poems of Octavio Paz, 1957–1987*. Both facts suggest to us that Paz did not wish his poem to be read exclusively in the light of Mexican pre-Hispanic references, just as nobody would think of reading the poem as a purely autobiographical summary, although it does contain specific references to his personal history.

A further important prefatory item which we must take into account, which has often excited the attention of critics, is Paz's quotation of Gérard de Nerval's esoteric poem 'Arthémis.' Much attention has been devoted in this context to the number thirteen, which appears in the poem and, as the sum of twelve plus one in reference to our twelve-hour clock, is, much like the fifth sun of the calendar stone or the six initial-final verses of Paz's poem, a symbol of transcendence. In connection with the calendar stone, the importance of the number thirteen goes further still. John Fein, in his study of Paz's major poems, notes the pervasive importance of the number thirteen in the Aztec calendar (1986, p. 16), which is really a combination of two calendars, solar and lunar. The lunar calendar of divination, known as the *tonalpohualli* (count of days), consisted of thirteen months of twenty days, that is, 260 days in all. To this we may add the Aztec concept of the 'thirteenth heaven,' abode of the original dual godhead, at the summit of the world, which Jacques Soustelle describes in the following terms: 'At the origin of all being, even the birth of the gods, the ancient Mexicans imagined a primordial couple, *Ometecuhtli*, "lord of Duality," and *Omeciuatl*, "lady of Duality." They live at the top of the world, in the *thirteenth heaven*, "there where the air is very cold, delicate and icy." From their eternal fecundity all the gods and all men are born. By the time period which concerns us, these great divinities had become somewhat similar to monarchs who rule without governing.'[4]

If we look more closely at Nerval's poem, however, we will discover its utility as a European source of reference, counterbalancing the indigenous American references, to what can only be described as truly universal symbols. The quatrain that Paz quotes from Nerval's poem reads as follows:

> Le treizième revient ... c'est encore la première,
> et c'est toujours la seule – ou c'est le seul moment;
> car es-tu reine, ô toi, la première or dernière?
> es-tu roi, toi le seul ou le dernier amant? (SB:259; OP1:217)

> (The thirteenth returns ... it is the first again, / and it is always the only one – or the only moment; / for are you queen, you, the first or last? / are you king, you the only or the last lover?)

The number symbolism, the concentration of time in the revelation of the instant and the 'yo'–'tú' dialogue that we explored in the previous chapter all are elements of meaning which would constitute more than sufficient reason for this quotation. From a Jungian perspective, however, it is not hard to find in the queen and king mentioned here echoes of the 'chymical wedding' of Rex and Regina in alchemical thought, which on the spiritual plane represents regeneration and the union of the Godhead and the Virgin Mother from which the redeemer is born (as well as the mystical marriage of Christ and the Church) and, on the physical plane, the union of Sol and Luna as the light and dark sides of Nature. The process of regeneration and renewal associated with the King is depicted in Ripley's *Cantilena* and Rosencreutz's *Chymical Wedding*, but, as Jung points out, it recurs in many different versions. The symbolism moves beyond sun and moon in the union of opposites to include also Venus, as can be appreciated in the following story, quoted by Jung from Salomon Trismosin's *Splendor solis*, which is the third *tractatus* of his *Aureum vellus*:

> The old Philosophers declared they saw a Fog rise, and pass over the whole face of the earth, they also saw the impetuosity of the Sea, and the streams over the face of the earth, and how these same became foul and stinking in the darkness. They further saw the king of the Earth sink, and heard him cry out with eager voice, 'Whosoever saves me shall live and reign with me for ever in my brightness on my royal throne,' and Night enveloped all things. The day after, they saw over the King an apparent Morning Star, and the light of Day clear up the darkness, and bright Sunlight pierce through the clouds, with manifold coloured rays of brilliant brightness, and a sweet perfume from the earth, and the Sun shining clear. Herewith was completed the Time when the King of the Earth was released and renewed, well apparelled, and quite handsome, surprising with his beauty the Sun and Moon. He was crowned with three costly crowns, the one of Iron, the other of Silver, and the third of pure Gold. They saw in his right hand a Sceptre with Seven Stars, all of which gave a golden Splendour. (1963, pp. 331–2)

The regal symbolism of the crowns and sceptre of seven stars, while perhaps immediately reminiscent of Christian apocalyptic imagery, should not blind us to the parallel with the Venusian cycle of descent and ascent of the Mexican man-god Quetzalcoatl, which, as we have already said, is the very stuff of *Piedra de sol.* The circularity of the thrones of the King and Queen and their association with a sacred calendar and Time is explicit in a rather different and medieval vision of these symbolic figures, the vision of paradise of the Norman prior and poet Guillaume de Digulleville in his *Pélérinage de l'âme* (quite distinct from that of Dante). Jung describes the content as follows:

> In the highest heaven of pure gold the King sits on a round throne which shines more brightly than the sun. A *couronne* of precious stones surrounds him. Beside him, on a circular throne that is made of brown crystal, sits the Queen, who intercedes for the sinners ... 'Raising his eyes to the golden heaven, the pilgrim perceived a marvellous circle which appeared to be three feet across. It came out of the golden heaven at one point and re-entered it at another, and it made the whole tour of the golden heaven.' This circle is sapphire-coloured. It is a small circle, three feet in diameter, and evidently it moves over a great horizontal circle like a rolling disc. This great circle intersects the golden circle of heaven. (1953a, p. 210)

The angel guiding the pilgrim protagonist then explains:

> Ce cercle que tu vois est le calendrier
> Qui en faisant son tour entier,
> Montre des Saints les journées
> Quand elles doivent être fêtées.
> Chacun en fait le cercle un tour,
> Chacune étoile y est pour jour,
> Chacun soleil pour l'espace
> De jours trente ou zodiaque. (ibid.)[5]

Whether it be zodiac, calendar of saints, or *tonalpohualli,* the circularity of the ritual calendar is the same.

In short, the symbols of *Piedra de sol* are universal symbols, and it is to this fact that the syncretism of references to Mexican and European tradition points. Fein's clarification (1986, p. 14) of the mystery of Nerval's hermetic poem through reference to Onimus's explanation of the impression made on Nerval by a certain ornate Renaissance pendulum clock has the interest of anecdotal fact, but does not circumvent the underlying importance of the symbolic associations of the poem. Despite Fein's supposition that the poem's significance for Paz did not lie in its mythological association (p. 15), he goes on to show the importance of the figure of Diana-Artemis by relating her to earlier goddesses, notably Isis, and by showing her relationship to Venus. The feminine deity wears a series of different faces throughout the passage of time, just as the female 'tú' figure in Paz's poem bears multiple names:

> Eloísa, Perséfona, María,
> muestra tu rostro al fin para que vea
> mi cara verdadera. (SB:276; OP1:231)

> (Heloise, Persephone, Mary, / show your face finally so I may see / my true countenance.)

It is clear from these very names that Paz is neither locked in a world of individual, personal references, nor exclusively concerned with a single cultural tradition. Though every element of *Piedra de sol* tends towards the unity of a coherent whole,[6] this is not achieved through a homogeneity of cultural reference but through a synthesis of disparate references based on the fundamental underlying similarity of collective symbolism.

The symbols of *Piedra de sol* and Nerval's poem are ancient and enduring. The symbolism of both the King and the goddess Diana hark back to Egyptian times, if not earlier. Jung also mentions, in this frame of reference, the association with Isis and Osiris, the divinity of the Pharoah, and the persistence, almost to modern times, of the divine right of kings.

The archetypal images of *Piedra de sol*

Piedra de sol, as our exploration of the prefatory material suggests, deals with time and the individual's birth into time. Birth is not seen in purely physical and social terms through a mere enumeration of concrete details of Paz's biography, but happens also on spiritual and psychological planes. In psychoanalytical terms, the poem can be said to depict the emergence of ego-consciousness from the unconscious totality of the pre-self and the ensuing struggle to integrate the self. As such, we may expect to find in it the traditional archetypes of individuation, notably the Great Mother and the anima, and several critics have commented on these. Nevertheless, we should begin with a more central image, that of the mandala, the sacred circular image of unity and centred symmetry, used in eastern religions for meditation and whose psychological characteristics are described at length by Jung in his 1950 essay 'Concerning mandala symbolism' (see Jung 1959a) as well as in a section of his earlier (1936) essay/lecture series 'Individual dream symbolism in relation to alchemy' (see Jung 1953a) devoted to the same subject. In a later article he gives the following summary description of the mandala symbol: 'The Sanscrit word *mandala* means "circle" in the ordinary sense of the word. In the sphere of religious practices and in psychology it denotes circular images, which are drawn, painted, modeled or danced. Plastic structures of this kind are to be found, for instance, in Tibetan Buddhism, and as dance figures these circular patterns occur also in Dervish monasteries. As psychological phenomena they appear spontaneously in dreams, in certain states of conflict, and in cases of schizophrenia. Very frequently they contain a quaternity or a multiple of four, in the form of a cross, a star, a square, an octagon, etc. In alchemy we encounter this motif in the form of *quadratura circuli*' (1959a, p. 387).[7]

The alchemical *quadratura circuli* or 'squaring of the circle' is one of two fundamental psychological processes associated with the mandala,[8] and sometimes described as separate archetypes: it is the integration of a quaternity or four points of reference within the circle as a symbol of psychic integration or wholeness. The other process is the journey towards the centre in search of the self, and in this regard the mandala is a symbol of the self. In fact, it is difficult to dissociate these two: both are present in the Aztec sun stone, since the Toltec-Aztec tradition, like many ancient eastern cosmogonies and unlike western traditions, recognized five cardinal points, the fifth being a centre rising like a vertical column in the centre of the world from the lowest regions of 'hell,' or the land of the dead, up to the thirteenth or highest sphere of heaven. Both are also present in the poetic movement of *Piedra de sol*, symbolized by the sum of the vertical upward surge of the fountain in the centre and the horizontal circular flow of the river, as depicted in the first and last six lines of the poem. Quaternity is prominent in Paz's major mandala, *Blanco*, but the very title of this poem suggests also the quest for the centre of totality and nothingness, the 'white' centre representing both the sum and absence of colours and the 'target' of the poetic experience. All of Paz's later long poems, explored in Phase Four, concern a circular journey in search of a centre and in that sense are more directly concerned with the plenitude of the self.

To return to Jung's 1936 essay and the Aztec sun stone: the latter is, in fact, included among Jung's illustrations as one of the most noteworthy mandalas from world religious art (1953a, p. 98), although it warrants only the most fleeting of references in Jung's actual commentary. Paz is, of course, fully aware of the form and significance of the mandala from his knowledge of Indian religion and culture, and some critics of Paz, such as Leticia Underwood, have taken up the topic in relation to *Piedra de sol*: she examines the mandala qualities of the sun stone in some detail (1992, pp. 83ff).[9] It is worth remarking, moreover, that the Renaissance clock which, as noted above, apparently fascinated Nerval and motivated his composition of 'Arthémis,' is another mandala symbol entirely parallel to that of the sun stone. Its significance is very close to that of the pendulum clock and the world clock appearing in the dreams analysed by Jung in *Psychology and Alchemy*.[10]

Frances Chiles notes that *Piedra de sol* 'is the perfect example of what Frye calls the pictorial or emblem poem, in which "the pictorial shape of the subject is suggested in the shape of the lines of the poem"' (1987, p. 103). This underlines an important aspect of the mandala image in relation to Paz's poetry: the pictorial quality by which structure becomes a direct reflection of meaning. In this sense, most of Paz's major poems, notably *Piedra de sol, Blanco,* and *Vuelta,* are mandalas. A second significant aspect is the sacred and ritual function that Paz ascribes to poetry. In *Piedra de sol* the mandala relates to the self, born out of the interaction of ego consciousness and cosmic and primeval natural unity, and to the great circular movement of time. In fact, mandalas for Paz always relate to time – circular time, poetic time, the time of truth, plenitude, and communion – and the mandala's dynamic function should be stressed as a symbol of both movement and constancy. The structure of *Piedra de sol,* on which most critical commentary has concentrated, yields only part of its meaning. Our movement through it as readers, as well as the movement of the poetic subject, produce a more essential signification.

These comments demonstrate the close relation of the mandala image in this poem with the *uroboros* or 'Great Round' archetype (cf. Neumann 1955, p. 18), which commonly assumes the form of a serpent biting its own tail. The uroboros symbolizes the undifferentiated initial psychic state in which positive and negative, male and female, conscious and unconscious, light and dark elements coexist. In the case of the sun stone, the double descending serpent which nevertheless encircles the cosmos is an interesting image of the emergence of temporal consciousness from the unconscious and a conscious (verbal?) linking of the two opposing faces through their tongues. The symbolization of the union of opposites in and through time would seem to be quite evident here. Can one see in the linking of tongues a suggestion that such union is achieved through communication?

Further light can be shed upon this dualistic symbol of union by comparing it to mercurial symbols in alchemy as described by Jung. Hermes or Mercurius is, of course, still symbolized by a popular and ancient image of the double entwined serpent. The alchemists saw him and his physical substance (quicksilver) as an image of transformation, union, regeneration and, as Gerhard Dorn would have it, 'the true hermaphroditic Adam and Microcosm': 'Our Mercurius is therefore that same [Microcosm] who contains within him the perfections, virtues, and powers of Sol [in the dual sense of sun and gold], and who goes through the streets and houses of all the planets, and in his regeneration has obtained the power of Above and Below, wherefore he is to be likened to their marriage' (quoted by Jung, 1963, p. 16). The 'power of Above and Below' stems from the fact that, as Jung explains, 'In alchemy Mercurius is the "ligament" of the soul, uniting spirit and body. His dual nature enables him to play the role of mediator; he is bodily and spiritual and is himself the union of these two principles' (p. 443). In more physical terms, his androgynous nature partakes of both the dark, masculine qualities of sulphur and the light, lunar, and feminine qualities of Sol (p. 184). Jung further notes: 'Mercurius is conceived as 'spiritual blood,' on the analogy of the blood of Christ' (p. 14), though he is also a diabolical figure associated with the serpent and darkness (see p. 185). The symbolic parallels between Mercury, Christ, and Quetzalcoatl now become apparent, and it is clear that three differing cultural traditions are united by the same universal primordial images at the unconscious level.

Commentary on the poem

Piedra de sol, we have postulated, traces in psychological terms the birth of ego-consciousness and depicts the process in terms of the universal creation myths described by Neumann (1954). The poem uses the myths of creation, notably Meso-American ones, to describe the birth of the individual into consciousness. Before we begin the commentary on the poem, it is good to remind ourselves of the precarious nature of creation in the view of the ancient Mexicans, for whom every genesis courted disaster and life always hung in the balance of fate determined by the struggle of the cosmic forces of light and darkness. There is no handiwork of an omnipotent god, or overpowering redemption of a saviour, as in the

Judeo-Christian tradition. Soustelle (1967) gives an apt description of the story of the five suns as depicted in the calendar stone:

> In the centre of the enormous stone disc known as the Aztec Calendar stone, a symbol in the form of a cross of Saint Andrew frames the grimacing face of the Sun. Four smaller discs accompany it. The whole assembly reads: *naui-ollin*, 'Four-Movement,' and it is the name of our world, 'ours, the one we inhabit, and which was also that of Our Lord of Tula, the Plumed Serpent.'
>
> The word *ollin*, incidentally, means both 'movement' and 'earthquake,' and it is the name of one of the twenty days of the Mexican sacred calendar. Our universe was born on the day 'Four-Movement,' when the Sun began to move in the skies, and its end will come among earthquakes and cataclysms. Then the monsters of dusk, the Tzitzimimé with skeleton masks hidden in the shadows of the West, waiting for their moment, will spring forth from the darkness to exterminate humanity.[11]

Soustelle goes on to outline the four suns preceding our current epoch of the fifth sun. In the first creation, *Naui-Ocelotl* (Four-Jaguar), men were devoured by jaguars, symbols of the forces of the earth. In the second, *Naui-Ehecatl* (Four-Wind), a storm put paid to creation, transforming men into monkeys. The third sun, *Naui-Quiauitl* (Four-Rain), saw the world engulfed in a rain of fire. *Naui-Atl* (Four-Water), was the fourth sun, which came to its end in a flood which only one human couple survived. Quetzalcoatl had to descend to the netherworld to revive the bones of the ancient dead through shedding his own blood for the current race of humanity to be born. It is not difficult for the westerner to recognize in these four suns the successive predominance of the four elements: earth, air, fire, and water. Creation in the indigenous Mexican world was an unfolding, ongoing process, in which the individual played a vital part through blood sacrifice. The sun, to advance along its course, needed the vital impulse of human blood, and thus humankind had a role to play in cosmic destiny. This vision of humanity and the universe shares certain ancient images with the western Christian tradition, but it is diametrically opposed to the latter's notion of consummated sacrifice.

Paz partakes, then, of a tradition in which individual fate is bound up with the world's fate. His personal history is related to that of the world in general, not in some egocentric act of hubris, but as an expression of moral responsibility. The life force that he proclaims in *Piedra de sol* is not the blood sacrifice of his ancestors, however, but the force of love and human solidarity. Nevertheless, blood is an important symbol throughout the poem, as we shall see.

The initial six verses of the poem are identical to the last six and end in a colon, thus stressing the poem's circular structure and perpetual, unfinished cycle. In them we find water images on a double horizontal-vertical plane:

un sauce de cristal, un chopo de agua,
un alto surtidor que el viento arquea,
un árbol bien plantado mas danzante,
un caminar de río que se curva,
avanza, retrocede, da un rodeo
y llega siempre: (SB:259–60; OP1:217)

(a willow-tree of crystal, a poplar-tree of water, / a tall fountain jet curved by the wind, / a tree firmly planted yet dancing, / a flowing of river in a curve, / forwards, backwards, in a meander / constantly arriving:)

The first three verses give us the vertical image of the fountain made concrete in the form of a tree (the sacred tree being an image of increasing importance in Paz's poetry from *La estación violenta* onward, as we shall see in later chapters). The jet of water rises from below and is curled over by the wind before falling to earth again like the leaves of the willow tree. The horizontal image of the river appears in the last three verses, running forwards, backwards, and finally describing a circle before pushing relentlessly onward. The two images may be related, through entirely traditional associations, to the themes of the unconscious and time. The two are interrelated and possessed of circular movement.

As we earlier noted in our comments on *Piedra de sol* as mandala, the movement of the poetic discourse exactly mirrors these emblems of movement. The whole poem can be seen as a constant welling up of images from the unconscious to illuminate the unceasingly repeatable kaleidoscopic treadmill path of conscious being. The process of constantly arriving ('llega siempre') is verbalized in a flow of repeated syntactic categories and structures which move effortlessly, like the poetic 'I' or centre of consciousness, from one open-ended stanza to another:

un caminar tranquilo
de estrella o primavera sin premura,
agua que con los párpados cerrados
mana toda la noche profecías,

unánime presencia en oleaje,
ola tras ola hasta cubrirlo todo,
verde soberanía sin ocaso
como el deslumbramiento de las alas
cuando se abren en mitad del cielo ...
un caminar entre las espesuras. (SB:260; OP1:217)

(a tranquil movement / of star or spring at measured pace, / water with closed eyelids / pouring prophecies all night long, / unanimous surging presence, / wave upon all-pervading wave, / sovereign unfading green / like the light-flash of wings / opening in the open sky ... / a movement through the thick undergrowth.)

None of the stanzas (of irregular length, like the *laisses* of epic poems of old) ends in a period, and most end in a comma, indicating continuity into the next stanza. As already noted, the final six lines end in a colon, indicating union with the beginning of the poem as it describes its vast circle. Though several critics have attempted to divide the poem into different sections to interpret its progress,[12] its very constant movement, the elemental *ollin*, convinces us that it should be read as a flowing whole. Jung would have described it as the *perpetuum mobile* to which he often has occasion to refer in his writings on dream analysis (1953a, pp. 105, 181, 222). *Ollin* and perpetual movement connote immortality. As Jung notes, 'immortality is a clock that never runs down, a mandala that revolves eternally like the heavens' (p. 181). Immortality or eternal continuity, then, is the backdrop against which Paz seeks to achieve his birth of ego-consciousness. As individual, personal discourse, the poem follows a spiral movement which reflects the rhythms of the unconscious in exactly the way described by Jung: 'We can hardly escape the feeling that the unconscious process moves spiral-wise round a centre, gradually getting closer, while the characteristics of the centre grow more and more distinct. Or perhaps we could put it the other way round and say that the centre – itself virtually unknowable – acts like a magnet on the disparate materials and processes of the unconscious and gradually captures them as in a crystal lattice' (p. 217).

In summary, the circular movement and the constant welling-up of the unconscious into the conscious give the lie to the linear exposition which we are about to undertake. There is no single development or advance, no succession of times or places in *Piedra de sol*, since each step forward is also a step backward, each projection is also a memory and every here and now reflects a there and then. In this respect, Victoria Carpenter's remarks on the non-linearity of time in her personal reading of the poem are most pertinent. She questions other critics' observations on standard time and timelessness and concludes that 'it is inaccurate to speak of timelessness in the course of the poem; there is a multiplicity of time(s) rather than its absence' (2001, p. 497). The twenty different time planes she then goes on to identify are related to the essential fact that the poem's sequentiality is dream-like rather than rooted in 'objective' reality: 'the reading of "Piedra de sol" as a dream sequence is supported by modern research on the meaning of dreams' (p. 498). Her first quoted and major source in this respect is Carl Jung.

Given the non-linear characteristics of the poem mentioned above, our method of exposition will, no doubt, sometimes seem forced and incomplete. It is simply a convenient fiction which we follow for the sake of clarity, but a fiction all the same.

The poem begins, as we see, with no presence of any discernible individual subject, but rather movement itself designated by the impersonal infinitive 'caminar.' In the Spanish infinitive particularly, verb and noun are still one, without conjugated form. Before the world begins, all presence is unanimous, unseparated, non-individual, and the image of water with its closed eyelids is a clear emblem of the unconscious. The movement of the Spirit over the waters is a luminous flash of wings.[13]

The journey through time still is, at the beginning of the second stanza, only a premonition, but the third takes up the theme of evil fate, hanging like a threat over the future:

> un caminar entre las espesuras
> de los días futuros y el aciago
> fulgor de la desdicha como un ave
> petrificando el bosque con su canto
> y las felicidades inminentes
> entre las ramas que se desvanecen,
> horas de luz que pican ya los pájaros,
> presagios que se escapan de la mano. (SB:260; OP1:217)

(a movement through the thick undergrowth / of future days and the fateful / glimmer of misfortune like a bird / turning the wood to stone with its song / and the premonitions of happiness / between the disappearing branches, / hours of light pecked away by birds, / presages slipping from one's grasp.)

The density of the primeval forest depicted in this stanza seems indicative of the unconscious depths from which arise the first stirrings of consciousness, possessed already of a tragic sense of life and destiny. Both the forest with its birds, and the water images of the previous stanza are probably better described as 'pre-creational' than as 'paradisiacal,' which is the adjective that Fein uses in consonance with his desire to view the first half of the poem as associated with the east and rebirth and resurrection (1986, pp. 23–4). In Jungian terms, though, all the images have a common association with a pre-conscious uroboric state and with the archetype of the Great Mother. The tone of sadness pervading this stanza is well described by Neumann as a condition of emergent consciousness: 'For the dawning light of consciousness, the maternal uroboros turns to darkness and night. The passage of time and the problem of death become a dominant life-feeling; Bachofen describes the mother-born, who know that they are born only of earth and mother, as being "sad by nature," for decay and the necessity of death are one side of the uroboros just because its other side signifies birth and life. The world wheel, the humming loom of time, the Weird Sisters, and the wheel of birth and death, all these symbols express the sadness that rules over the life of the adolescent ego' (1954, p. 45).

The fourth stanza brings the sudden innovation of a presence. Dry land is separated from the waters, is envisaged as the luminous presence of a female body. Air, fire, and earth supplant water as the elemental forces in the unfolding creation:

> una presencia como un canto súbito,
> como el viento cantando en el incendio,
> una mirada que sostiene en vilo
> al mundo con sus mares y sus montes,
> cuerpo de luz filtrada por un ágata,
> piernas de luz, vientre de luz, bahías,
> roca solar, cuerpo color de nube,
> color de día rápido que salta,
> la hora centellea y tiene cuerpo,
> el mundo ya es visible por tu cuerpo,
> es transparente por tu transparencia. (SB:260; OP1:217–8)

(a presence like a sudden song, / like the wind singing in the fire, / a gaze holding the world / with its seas and mountains up to view, / body of light filtered through an agate stone, / legs of light, belly of light, bays, / solar rock, body colour of cloud, / colour of swift springing day, / the hour sparkles and is embodied, / the world becomes visible through your body, / transparent through your transparency.)

Pronouns are born with the appearance of the second-person 'tú'; the world passes from premonition to presence in the broadest, most undifferentiated figure of the female other: the Great Mother.[14] The archetypal 'tú' paves the way for the first appearance of the as yet unborn poetic subject: 'yo.' The image of the presence of the 'tú' as a 'sudden song' and the advance of the 'yo' through 'galleries of sound' suggest a parallel between cosmic and poetic creation. Yet word and sound are not enough to give, as yet, a fixed identity to the 'yo,' who constantly disappears and re-emerges in the transparent mirrors of the spirit:

voy entre galerías de sonidos,
fluyo entre las presencias resonantes,
voy por las transparencias como un ciego,
un reflejo me borra, nazco en otro,
oh bosque de pilares encantados,[15]
bajo los arcos de la luz penetro
los corredores de un otoño diáfano. (SB:260–1; OP1:218)

(I go through galleries of sound, / I flow between resonating presences, / I advance blindly through translucencies, / I disappear in one reflection and am born in the next, / oh forest of enchanted pillars, / beneath the arches of light I enter / the corridors of a diaphanous autumn.)

Over the next few stanzas the moving poetic subject discovers the dimensions of the 'tú,' first as a space of city and landscape:

eres una ciudad que el mar asedia,
una muralla que la luz divide
en dos mitades de color durazno,
un paraje de sal, rocas y pájaros
bajo la ley del mediodía absorto. (SB:261; OP1:218)

(you are a city besieged by the sea, / a wall divided by the light / in two halves the colour of peach, / a place of salt and rocks and birds / under the law of an engrossed midday.)

Then she appears as a goddess figure, with typical Mexican associations in her guise as Coatlicue, 'Lady of the Serpent Skirt,' mother of the gods and goddess of rebirth, who partakes of both the dark nature of the earth ('los tigres') and the fiery nature of the solar hummingbird:[16]

> los tigres beben sueño en esos ojos,
> el colibrí se quema en esas llamas,
> ...
> tu falda de maíz ondula y canta. (SB:261; OP1:218)

(tigers drink sleep in those eyes, / the hummingbird is burned in those flames ... / your skirt of maize flutters and sings.)

The operative word for the 'yo' is 'voy.' He is the possessor of *ollín*, primal movement:

> voy entre galerías de sonidos ...
> voy por las transparencias como un ciego ...
> voy por tu cuerpo como por el mundo ...
> voy por tus ojos como por el agua ...
> voy por tu frente como por la luna ...
> voy por tu talle como por un río ...
> voy por tu cuerpo como por un bosque ...
> voy por tus pensamientos afilados. (SB:260–1; OP1:218–19; emphasis ours)

(I go through galleries of sound ... / I advance blindly through translucencies ... / I move through your body as through the world ... / I move through your eyes as through water ... / I move through your forehead as through the moon ... / I move through your waistline as through a river ... / I move through your body as through a forest ... / I move through your sharp thoughts.)

The 'yo' as active spirit 'creates' the 'tú' as a mentally projected essence:

> vestida del color de mis deseos
> como mi pensamiento vas desnuda. (SB:261; OP1:218)

(dressed in the colour of my desire / like my thought you walk naked)

And the 'tú' as body and earth-womb gives birth to the 'yo.' The process of birth and creation is thus viewed in *Piedra de sol* as a dialectic rather than simply as the fusion of opposites and the resolution of paradox that we have explored in Paz's earlier poetry. The fusion of opposites is embodied in the duality of the goddess herself. She is both land and sea, solid presence and liquid dream flow, two parts of a wall divided by light:[17]

eres una ciudad que el mar asedia,
una muralla que la luz divide
en dos mitades de color durazno. (SB:261; OP1:218)

(you are a city besieged by the sea, / a wall divided by the light / in two halves the colour of peach.)

Slowly the dark, female *yin* identity predominates in the succession of images of moon, cloud and womb, and the liquid images of before reappear:

tu falda de cristal, tu falda de agua,
tus labios, tus cabellos, tus miradas,
toda la noche llueves, todo el día
abres mi pecho con tus dedos de agua,
cierras mis ojos con tu boca de agua,
sobre mis huesos llueves, en mi pecho
hunde raíces de agua un árbol líquido,

voy por tu talle como por un río,
voy por tu cuerpo como por un bosque. (SB:261–2; OP1:218–9)

(your skirt of crystal, your skirt of water, / your lips, your hair, your gaze, / all night long your rain falls, all day long / you open my breast with your fingers of water, / you close my eyes with your lips of water, / you rain down upon my bones, in my breast / a liquid tree takes root, / I move through your waistline as through a river, / I move through your body as through a forest.)

The 'yo' regresses to the unconscious state, the goddess reverts to the Earth Mother and to the already familiar images of fountain or tree of water ('árbol líquido'), river, and forest. It is as if we had here the personification of the images contained in the initial six lines of the poem.

The meanderings of the 'yo' along the oniric river end suddenly in an abrupt descent, an abortive birth into disintegration and solitude:

voy por tu talle como por un río,
voy por tu cuerpo como por un bosque,
como por un sendero en la montaña
que en un abismo brusco se termina,
voy por tus pensamientos afilados
y a la salida de tu blanca frente
mi sombra despeñada se destroza,
recojo mis fragmentos uno a uno
y prosigo sin cuerpo, busco a tientas. (SB:262; OP1:219)

(I move through your waistline as through a river, / I move through your body as through a forest, / as along a path on the mountainside / which ends abruptly in an abyss, / I move through your sharp thoughts, / and on emerging from your white forehead / my shadow falling headlong shatters on the ground, / I pick up my pieces bit by bit / and walk on without a body, groping.)

The 'yo' emerges from the forehead of the 'tú': just as she is his mental projection, so he is hers. As the creative process begins to take shape, so also does the way it is informed by myth, in particular the legend of the five suns. Creation for the Aztecs is a necessarily repeatable, perfectible process. For Paz and the psychological interpretation of his poem, the human being must be born and reborn again and again, until s/he transcends solitude. The 'yo' is born as a mere shadow, a being desperately searching to reunite its fragments, a subject without body: the verb 'busco' supplants 'voy.'

The galleries of mirrors reappear, this time as corridors of memory, where time stagnates and images of drought, death and decay prevail:

corredores sin fin de la memoria,
puertas abiertas a un salón vacío
donde se pudren todos los veranos,
las joyas de la sed arden al fondo,
rostro desvanecido al recordarlo,
mano que se deshace si la toco,
cabelleras de arañas en tumulto
sobre sonrisas de hace muchos años. (SB:262; OP1:219)

(endless corridors of memory, / doors open upon an empty room / where all the summers lie rotting, / and at the back the jewels of thirst burn, / a face which fades away upon remembrance, / a hand which crumbles at my touch, / spider hair in disarray / covering smiles from many years ago.)

This wasteland is uninhabited: open doors lead into empty rooms, and the search that the 'yo' has undertaken yields nothing:

busco sin encontrar, escribo a solas,
no hay nadie, cae el día, cae el año,
caigo con el instante, caigo a fondo. (SB:262; OP1:219)

(I search and find not, I write alone, / there is no one, the day falls, the year falls, / I fall with the moment, I fall to the depths.)

The moving, liquid presence of the goddess has vanished and the free fall of the 'yo' into concrete particularity continues:

caigo con el instante, caigo a fondo,
invisible camino sobre espejos
que repiten mi imagen destrozada,
piso días, instantes caminados,
piso los pensamientos de mi sombra,
piso mi sombra en busca de un instante. (SB:262; OP1:219)

(I fall with the moment, I fall to the depths, / invisible path over mirrors / which multiply my shattered image, / I tread upon days, already trodden instants, / I tread on the thoughts of my shadow, / I tread on my shadow in search of an instant.)

The blind awkwardness of the subject is palpable in the last line: 'I tread on my shadow in search of an instant.' Shadow has here, perhaps, a double meaning: on the one hand, the incarnate ego is but a shadow of his former self; on the other, the shadow represents all of the dark elements of unconscious self, accessible only with difficulty to ego-consciousness.

Eventually, though, the 'yo' begins to discover that presence can be recovered only through memory, through time made present, recovered time. Time is, in fact, the principle of movement in the human world, the dynamism able to restore each instantaneous scene or vision to its moment of plenitude:

busco una fecha viva como un pájaro,
busco el sol de las cinco de la tarde
templado por los muros de tezontle:
la hora maduraba sus racimos
y al abrirse salían las muchachas
de su entraña rosada y se esparcían
por los patios de piedra del colegio,
alta como el otoño caminaba
envuelta por la luz bajo la arcada
y el espacio al ceñirla la vestía
de una piel más dorada y transparente. (SB:263; OP1:220)

(I search for a date living like a bird, / I search for the five o'clock afternoon sun / tempered by tezontle walls: / the clusters of the hour ripened / and opened to let the girls come running / from their pink entrails and spread out / over the stone patios of the school, / tall as the autumn she walked / swathed in light under the arches / and the space encircling her body dressed her / with a more golden and transparent skin.)

An idyllic childhood memory of a girl emerging from a schoolyard leads the subject back into images of light, the fecundity of rain and mythical associations of the Mexican tradition (tiger, deer):

tigre color de luz, pardo venado
por los alrededores de la noche,
entrevista muchacha reclinada
en los balcones verdes de la lluvia. (SB:263; OP1:220)

(tiger colour of light, dun-coloured deer / through the night surroundings, / a reclining girl half glimpsed / upon the rain's green balconies.)

The face, recovered in time, becomes a plural one, an 'innumerable face,' a succession of what are clearly anima figures:

adolescente rostro innumerable,
he olvidado tu nombre, Melusina,
Laura, Isabel, Perséfona, María,
tienes todos los rostros y ninguno,
eres todas las horas y ninguna. (SB:263; OP1:220)

(innumerable adolescent face, / I have forgotten your name, Melusina, / Laura, Isabel, Persephone, Mary, / you have every face and none, / you are every hour and none.)

The diversity and complexity of the anima personae is striking. Persephone and Mary are mythic-religious figures from very different traditions, the former embodying perhaps the principle of rebirth, the latter perhaps that of transcendence. Laura and Isabel are more human figures, object of the devotions of two great love poets, Petrarch and Garcilaso. Melusina or Mélisande is, for her part, a hybrid figure, half-human, half-fairy, the very embodiment of duality in her beauteous and monstrous sides. Maybe Underwood is right in seeing herein a search for the eternal feminine: 'The poem alludes to a quasi-mystical experience – the search for the eternal feminine in "Piedra de sol" develops within the context of a play of opposites: woman is "saint or fée"' (1992, p. 77). In other words, the search for unification and the anima projections of the 'yo' are to be seen on the level of Man searching for Woman, rather than a man searching for a woman.

The figure of Melusina brings further dimensions to the male-female union which we explore later. In Paz's poem, as Mélusine or Mélisande, married to Raymond de Poitiers, she is consonant with other references to French folklore and literary tradition,[18] such as to the story of Heloïse (Eloisa) and Abelard. However, she is also a figure who was well known to the alchemists from Paracelsus on, and, as Jung notes, she is associated with the mercurial spirit:

In alchemy, the *spiritus mercurii* that lives in the tree is represented as serpent, salamander, or Melusina. We find the last-mentioned in the 'Ripley Scrowle,' where the lizard is half a woman and is celebrating the *conjunctio* (marriage) with the *filius philosophorum* ... The 'Verses belonging to an Emblematicall Scrowle' (Thetr. chem. Brit., p. 375) run as follows:

And Azot is truly my Sister,
And Kibrick forsooth is my Brother:
The Serpent of Arabia is my name,
The which is leader of all this game. (1953a, p. 458)

What follows from these references to anima figures over the next two stanzas of Paz's poem is a flood of mythical and cosmic images rising from the unconscious in what is truly one of the moments of highest poetic inspiration in *Piedra de sol*:

te pareces al árbol y a la nube,
eres todos los pájaros y un astro,
te pareces al filo de la espada
y a la copa de sangre del verdugo,
yedra que avanza, envuelve y desarraiga
al alma y la divide de sí misma,

escritura de fuego sobre el jade,
grieta en la roca, reina de serpientes,
columna de vapor, fuente en la peña,
circo lunar, peñasco de las águilas,
grano de anís, espina diminuta
y mortal que da penas inmortales,
pastora de los valles submarinos
y guardiana del valle de los muertos,
liana que cuelga del cantil del vértigo,
enredadera, planta venenosa,
flor de resurrección, uva de vida,
señora de la flauta y del relámpago,
terraza del jazmín, sal en la herida,
ramo de rosas para el fusilado,
nieve en agosto, luna del patíbulo,
escritura del mar sobre el basalto,
escritura del viento en el desierto,
testamento del sol, granada, espiga,

rostro de llamas, rostro devorado,
adolescente rostro perseguido
años fantasmas, días circulares
que dan al mismo patio, al mismo muro,
arde el instante y son un solo rostro
los sucesivos rostros de la llama,
todos los nombres son un solo nombre,
todos los rostros son un solo rostro,
todos los siglos son un solo instante
y por todos los siglos de los siglos
cierra el paso al futuro un par de ojos. (SB:263–4; OP1:220–1)

(you resemble tree and cloud, / you are all birds and a planet star, / you resemble the edge of the sword / and the cup of blood of the executioner,

/ ivy creeping, engulfing and uprooting / the soul, dividing it from itself, / writing of fire on jade, / crevice in the rock, queen of serpents, / pillar of mist, fountain in the cliff, / lunar circus, eagles' ridge, / aniseed, minute and mortal thorn, / bringing immortal sorrow, / shepherdess of underwater valleys / and guardian of the valley of the dead, / liana hanging on the edge of vertigo, / poisonous, climbing plant, / resurrection's flower, grape of life, / lady of the flute and lightning, / jasmine terrace, salt in the wound, / bunch of roses for the victim shot, / snow in August, gallows moon, / writing of sea on basalt, / writing of wind in the desert, / testament of sun, pomegranate, ear of corn, / face of flame, face devoured, / adolescent face pursued / ghosts of years, circles of days / all looking onto the same patio, the same wall, / all the same face in the burning instant / the successive faces in the flame, / all names are a single name, / all faces are a single face, / all centuries are a single instant / and throughout all centuries / the way to the future is blocked by a pair of eyes.)

The major mythical reference here is to Coatlicue, mother of the gods and, as we should particularly remember, mother of the sun god Huitzilopochtli. To a western imagination, Coatlicue is understood better as a cosmic process than as a persona, since her manifestations generally occur in conjunction with other goddesses, such as Chalchihuitlicue, 'goddess of the jade petticoat,' associated with Tlaloc and the rain gods, and Chicomecoatl, 'savage snake woman,' in charge of the nourishment of humankind. She can also be seen as a female counterpart to Quetzalcoatl himself, and she is thus associated with the cycle of Venus. In her representations appear the symbols of the entwined snakes and the moon (as, for instance, in the famous statue of her in the Mexican Museum of Anthropology). She is a supremely dualistic figure, representative of life merging with death and emerging from death. In her association with Xipe Totec, the god of spring, she is a reminder of the terrible and bloody sacrifice needed to maintain the cosmic order. So much for the underlying current of mythical references in these two stanzas. Coatlicue, as mother of the gods, is also an obvious cultural configuration of the Great Mother archetype, and the plethora of teeming images is largely feminine in content (queen, snake, crevice in the rock, pillar of mist, moon, flower, and so on). All flow in a synthetic movement towards a face, a face of fire perceived in the fire of the spirit, a face where all faces, names, and centuries merge. The image recalls that of the adolescent looking narcissistically at his own image in the water, in the initial pages of *El laberinto de la soledad.* In his search for meaning and inspiration through the figures of the anima, the 'yo' ultimately is led to a confrontation with himself, the other in the mirror. This image as individual projection blocks access to the future: 'cierra el paso al futuro un par de ojos.' It is a synthesis, a moment of fruition and understanding, but only one instant in the passage of time.

The particularly Mexican framework of reference in the stanzas above is underlined by the mention of jade and basalt, two stones commonly used in religious representation. What appears on both is writing: the writing of fire on jade, and of sea on basalt. Though this writing belongs more to the order of the cosmos and of nature than to human order, writing per se is the representation of meaning, the communication and preservation of sense as conceived by the conscious mind. The personal reference to Paz the poet in the stance of the solitary writer, struggling through the night to capture the images surging from the unconscious laboriously in words, letter by letter, is outlined in the following stanza, reminiscent of the initial section of *¿Águila o sol?* titled 'Trabajos del poeta,' written some eight years earlier in 1949:

no hay nada frente a mí, sólo un instante
rescatado esta noche, contra un sueño
de ayuntadas imágenes soñado,
duramente esculpido contra el sueño,
arrancado a la nada de esta noche,
a pulso levantado letra a letra,
mientras afuera el tiempo se desboca
y golpea las puertas de mi alma
el mundo con su horario carnicero. (SB:264; OP1:221)

(in front of me there is nothing, just a moment / salvaged tonight, from a dream / dreamed of images yoked together, / sculpted in hard letters upon the dream, / snatched from the emptiness of night, / laboriously pulled up letter by letter, / while outside time rushes round / and beats at the doors of my soul / the world with its bloodthirsty time schedule.)

The poet lives in alienation, his act of creation is out of step with the 'bloodthirsty time schedule' of the world outside. The beautiful structure of synthesis built up by inspiration comes crashing down. Memory fragments, the 'yo' grows old, his eyes dim, his blood runs slow, and time deteriorates into an abominable succession of empty years:

sólo un instante mientras las ciudades,
los nombres, los sabores, lo vivido,
se desmoronan en mi frente ciega,
mientras la pesadumbre de la noche
mi pensamiento humilla y mi esqueleto,
y mi sangre camina más despacio
y mis dientes se aflojan y mis ojos
se nublan y los días y los años
sus horrores vacíos acumulan. (SB:265; OP1:221)

(just an instant while the cities, / names, tastes, life's experiences, / crumble away in my blind forehead, / while night's sorrow / humbles my thought and my bones, / and my blood runs slower / and my teeth come loose and my eyes / cloud over and the days and years / pile up their empty horror.)

Only the magic instant of unity and fullness remains as a memory in the descent into death. Threatened on all sides by death and darkness, it grows inward, like a tree inside the 'yo,' a sacred tree whose branches are his veins (an image which will grow in importance in the later poetry of Paz). In psychological terms, this is quite literally an image of introversion,[19] whence the apt characterization of the tree as 'árbol mental':

el instante translúcido se cierra
y madura hacia dentro, echa raíces,
crece dentro de mí, me ocupa todo,
me expulsa su follaje delirante,
mis pensamientos sólo son sus pájaros,
su mercurio circula por mis venas,
árbol mental, frutos sabor de tiempo. (SB:265; OP1:222)

(the translucent moment closes / and matures inwards, casting down roots, / it grows inside me, filling my whole space, / its raving foliage expels me, / my thoughts are only its birds, / its mercury courses through my veins, / tree of mind, fruits tasting of time.)

The sap of the tree, the blood of the 'yo' is described as 'mercury': the inner tree conserves its transforming power. Jung describes mercury as signifying primarily a transforming substance or spirit for the alchemists:

'In alchemical writings the word "Mercurius" is used with a very wide range of meaning, to denote not only the chemical element mercury or quicksilver, Mercury (Hermes) the god, and Mercury the planet, but also – and primarily – the secret "transforming substance" which is at the same time the "spirit" indwelling in all living creatures' (1953a, p. 26).

Life becomes internalized, soul transmuted into spirit, and the female 'tú' wounds him, mystically carving red writing in his flesh. This is both a bloodletting, a sacrifice perhaps of purification for the quest, and an image for the distinctly alchemical process of red sulphur being extracted from the solar gold and seeking to be reunited with the white sulphur (represented in this case as 'salitre') and moisture of Luna:

> frente a la tarde de *salitre* y *piedra*
> armada de navajas invisibles
> una *roja* escritura indescifrable
> escribes en mi piel y esas heridas
> como un traje de *llamas* me recubren,
> *ardo* sin consumirme, *busco el agua*
> y en tus ojos no hay agua, son de *piedra*. (SB:266; OP1:222; emphasis ours)

> (opposite the afternoon of *saltpetre* and *stone* / armed with invisible knives / an undecipherable writing in *red* / you carve on my skin and these wounds / cover me like a suit of *flames* / I *burn* without being consumed, *I search for the water* / and in your eyes there is no water, they are *stone*.)

The problem for the *coniunctio* is that the female element has become non-transformable, lifeless stone.

To make these obscure alchemical references somewhat clearer, we may cite the following description of the *coniunctio* process given by Jung:

> The persons who enact the drama of this problem are man and woman, in alchemy King and Queen, Sol and Luna ...
>
> In alchemy, the sun signifies first of all gold. But just as the 'philosophical' gold is not the common 'gold,' so the sun is neither just the metallic gold nor the heavenly orb. Sometimes the sun is an active substance hidden in the gold and is extracted as the *tinctura rubea* (red tincture). Sometimes, as the heavenly body, it is the possessor of magically effective and transformative rays. As gold and a heavenly body it contains an active sulphur of a red colour, hot and dry. Because of this red sulphur the alchemi-

cal sun, like the corresponding gold, is red. As every alchemist knew, gold owes its red colour to the admixture of Cu (copper), which he interpreted as Kypris (the Cyprian, Venus), mentioned in Greek alchemy as the transformative substance. (1963, pp. 92–3)

As Jung later illustrates, the red 'transforming substance' as masculine principle and the feminine salt are two different 'spirits' of the arcane substance, reunited in the dual, hermaphroditic nature of mercury:[20] 'In my chapter on Sulphur I have pointed out that it, especially in its red form, is identical with gold, the latter being generally regarded as "rex." The red sceptre of the king might be an allusion to this. There is, as I have shown, a red and a white sulphur, so it too is duplex and identical with Mercurius. Red sulphur stands for the masculine, active principle of the sun, the white for that of the moon. As sulphur is generally masculine by nature and forms the counterpart of the feminine salt, the two figures probably signify the spirits of the arcane substance, which is often called rex, as in Bernardus Trevisanus' (pp. 506–7).

The remainder of the stanza that we are examining, certainly one of the most complex stanzas of the poem, refers simultaneously to the mercurial process of death and to corruption (poisoned time, stagnant well water, taste of dust) and transformation and regeneration, to which we shall return later, and to the sacrificial attitude of fascination of the 'yo' before the Great Mother, still seen as the goddess Coatlicue. Her external form is now just a stone image, but in the return to the uterine space projected mentally as her body, the 'yo' is again led as a blind man through galleries of mirrors towards the centre of the circle (the very place of the sun god himself on the Aztec calendar stone) and there sees her as primeval light or spirit, a 'flaying light' shaped in the form of a sacrificial axe. The act of flaying is here specifically associated with Coatlicue through Xipe Totec (the Aztec god of spring who bore the flayed skin of children as a symbol of youth and regeneration), but, as Jung points out, it is an ancient religious sacrificial tradition, ranging from the Dionysian mysteries in Greece to China and Patagonia (1967, pp. 70–1). The second sacrificial act is the removal of the heart:

y tus palabras afiladas cavan
mi pecho y me despueblan y vacían. (SB:266; OP1:223)

(and your sharp words dig into / my breast and empty and depopulate me.)

The 'yo' is blow by blow bereft of memory in an action of the Great Mother as sorceress, which cannot fail to evoke the Homeric image of Ulysses and his friends captive in the power of Circe:

> uno a uno me arrancas los recuerdos,
> he olvidado mi nombre, mis amigos
> gruñen entre los cerdos o se pudren
> comidos por el sol en un barranco. (SB:266; OP1:223)
>
> (one by one you tear away my memories, / I have forgotten my name, my friends / grunt among pigs or rot away / devoured by the sun in a ravine)

Neumann succinctly describes this function of the Great Mother: 'The Great Mother is therefore the sorceress who transforms men into animals – Circe, mistress of wild beasts, who sacrifices the male and rends him (1954, p. 61). And again:

> But this triple-bodied, uroboric Hecate, mistress of the three realms – sky, earth, and underworld – is the teacher of Circe and Medea in the arts of magic and destruction. To her is attributed the power to enchant and change men into animals, and to smite with madness, which gift belongs to her as to all moon-goddesses. The mysteries of the Great Mother were celebrated by women, peaceably enough in Eleusis, but in a sanguinary manner in the cult of Dionysus; and the orgiastic rending of goat and bull, with the eating of the bloody fragments as a symbolic act of fertilization, extends from Osiris to Dionysus-Zagreus and Orpheus, Pentheus, and Actaeon. As the Orphic saying has it, 'The victim must be torn asunder and devoured.' (p. 83)

The 'yo' is now reduced to emptiness, pure thought and a windowless present in the isolation of his own ego:

> no hay nada en mí sino una larga herida,
> una oquedad que ya nadie recorre,
> presente sin ventanas, pensamiento
> que vuelve, se repite, se refleja
> y se pierde en su misma transparencia,
> conciencia traspasada por un ojo
> que se mira mirarse hasta anegarse
> de claridad. (SB:266; OP1:223)

(There is nothing in me but a long wound, / an emptiness visited by no one, / a windowless present, a thought / recurrent, self-repeating, self-reflecting / losing itself in its own transparency, / consciousness penetrated by an eye / which looks at itself looking until it drowns / in clarity.)

The image of Melusina is now evoked again, and the monstrous view of her scales as mermaid or half-snake is described by the 'yo,' just as in the legend Raymond de Poitiers sees her, causing her to disappear forever. Melusina is the dialectic image of the feminine creating, and yet created by, man.

Both the 'yo' and the 'tú' are now ancient and decrepit:

y al cabo de los siglos me descubro
con tos y mala vista, barajando
viejas fotos:[21]
no hay nadie, no eres nadie,
un montón de ceniza y una escoba,
un cuchillo mellado y un plumero,
un pellejo colgado de unos huesos.[22] (SB:267; OP1:223)

(and at the end of the centuries I find myself / with a cough and poor eyesight, shuffling through / old photos: / nobody is there, you are nobody, / a pile of ash and a broom, / a jagged knife and feather duster, / a skin draped over a few old bones.)

The 'yo' asks himself whether the traditional 'mother' instinct of women can be a path for the man towards authentic life, or whether it is some kind of mortal snare. He longs to break out of the prison of himself and be a dream of the future in the eyes of the other, but he cannot transcend an imperfectly remembered past:

¡caer, volver, soñarme y que me sueñen
otros ojos futuros, otra vida,
otras nubes, morirme de otra muerte!
– esta noche me basta, y este instante
que no acaba de abrirse y revelarme
dónde estuve, quién fui, cómo te llamas,
cómo me llamo yo. (SB:267–8; OP1:224)

(to fall, return, dream of myself and be dreamt / by other future eyes, another life, / other clouds, to die another death! / – this night is enough for me, and this instant / which never quite opens and reveals to me / where I was, who I was, what your name is, / what mine is too.)

The 'yo,' old, frail, and mortal, devoid of all mythical and archetypal relations and perceptions, is now reduced quite literally to the personal history of Octavio Paz, Mexican poet of the twentieth century. There follows a list of personal and trivial details, formulated mainly in the form of questions and fragmented snatches of speech, reminiscent of Eliot's *The Waste Land* and *The Love Song of J. Alfred Prufrock*:[23]

¿hacía planes
para el verano – y todos los veranos –
en Christopher Street, hace diez años,
con Filis que tenia dos hoyuelos
donde bebían luz los gorriones?
¿por la Reforma Carmen me decía
'no pesa el aire, aquí siempre es octubre' (SB:268; OP1:224)

(Did I make plans / for the summer – and for every summer – / in Christopher Street, ten years ago, / with Phyllis and her two dimples / the sparrows drank light from? / did Carmen used to tell me along Reforma / 'the air is light, here it's always October'?)

Life becomes a meaningless ritual of repetition of names, places and streets, devoid of real human presence or contact; a faceless 'someone' combs her hair, sings, puts on her clothes:

nombres, sitios,
calles y calles, rostros, plazas, calles,
estaciones, un parque, cuartos solos,
manchas en la pared, alguien se peina,
alguien canta a mi lado, alguien se viste,
cuartos, lugares, calles, nombres, cuartos. (SB:268; OP1:225)

(names, places /streets and more streets, faces, squares, streets, / stations, a park, solitary rooms, / stains on the wall, someone combs her hair, / someone sings beside me, someone puts on her clothes, / rooms, places, streets, names, rooms.)

Suddenly, the monotonous, repetitious succession is broken by a single place and date: Madrid, 1937 (SB:268; OP1:225). We are at the mid or low point of the poem. Here, the poem is driven purely and simply by the personal experience of the individual, Octavio Paz, a poet born in Mexico City in 1914, who as a young poet witnessed the horrors of the Spanish Civil War and the nobility of human solidarity and sacrifice which it produced. The poet recalls a scene where two people make love in the midst of a bombing attack on the Spanish capital, when it suddenly becomes apparent to him that through love and human solidarity, time may be conquered and our alienated present transcended:

los dos se desnudaron y se amaron
por defender nuestra porción eterna,
nuestra ración de tiempo y paraíso,
tocar nuestra raíz y recobrarnos,
recobrar nuestra herencia arrebatada
por ladrones de vida hace mil siglos,
los dos se desnudaron y besaron
porque las desnudeces enlazadas
saltan el tiempo y son invulnerables,
nada las toca, vuelven al principio,
no hay tú ni yo, mañana, ayer ni nombres,
verdad de dos en sólo un cuerpo y alma,
oh ser total. (SB:269; OP1:225)

(the two took off their clothes and made love / to defend our portion of eternity, / our ration of time and paradise, / to go back to our roots and recover ourselves, / recover our inheritance snatched from us / by thieves of life a thousand centuries ago, / the two took off their clothes and kissed / because two naked beings intertwined / transcend time and are invulnerable, / nothing touches them, they return to the beginning, / where there is no you nor I, tomorrow, yesterday or names, / dual truth in a single body and soul, / oh total being.)

Love is a revolutionary act, a return to lost paradise, to the beginning. The 'tú' and 'yo' fuse into a new truth of body and soul, of total being. The *coniunctio* is possible, not through a mental, inward odyssey, but through our immanence in time and space, in our historical, material being. In the mortal leap towards the other, the individual is reborn and transforms the world. The segregated urban spaces of rooms and streets which in an earlier stanza we described as a monotonous, repetitive succession are caught up now in a liquid flood of energy, the mercurial water of transformation which at last flows in abundance:

cuartos a la deriva
entre ciudades que se van a pique,
...
cuartos que son navíos que se mecen
en un golfo de luz; o submarinos:
el silencio se esparce en olas verdes. (SB:269; OP1:225–6)

(rooms adrift / among cities sinking in the water ... / rooms which are ships swaying / in a gulf of light, or submarines: / silence spreads in green waves.)

The transformation is a transfiguration of light and lightness, air and openness, fruition and fertility:

todo lo que tocamos fosforece;
mausoleos del lujo, ya roídos
los retratos, raídos los tapetes;
trampas, celdas, cavernas encantadas,
pajareras y cuartos numerados,
todos se transfiguran, todos vuelan,
cada moldura es nube, cada puerta
da al mar, al campo, al aire, cada mesa
es un festín; cerrados como conchas
el tiempo inútilmente los asedia,
no hay tiempo ya, ni muro: ¡espacio, espacio,
abre la mano, coge esta riqueza,
corta los frutos, come de la vida,
tiéndete al pie del árbol, bebe el agua! (SB:269–70; OP1:226)

(all we touch is set aglow; / mausoleums of luxury with weathered / portraits, threadbare rugs; / traps, cells, enchanted caverns, / birdcages and numbered rooms, / all are transfigured, all take flight, / every moulding becomes a cloud, every door / opens on to the sea, the countryside, the fresh air, every table / bears a banquet; closed like shells / time in vain lays siege to them, / there is no time anymore, nor walls: space! space! / open your hand, grasp these riches, / pluck the fruits, eat from life, / lie down at the foot of the tree, drink the water!)

The transfiguration as revolution, return to Eden, is an irruption of the sacred into daily mundane existence, since man and woman joining in a kiss become the original couple, creators of the world:

todo se transfigura y es sagrado,
es el centro del mundo cada cuarto,
es la primera noche, el primer día,
el mundo nace cuando dos se besan,
gota de luz de entrañas transparentes. (SB:270; OP1:226)

(all is transfigured and made sacred, / every room is the centre of the world, / the first night, the first day, / the world is born when two kiss, / a drop of light from transparent inner beings.)

The whole hypocritical theatre of the roles and distinctions of society, described in a list of bestial caricatures, all of the 'máscaras podridas / que dividen al hombre de los hombres' comes crashing down, and for an eternal moment we catch a glimpse of our lost unity, the plenitude of human identity and existence:

las máscaras podridas
que dividen al hombre de los hombres,
al hombre de sí mismo,
se derrumban
por un instante inmenso y vislumbramos
nuestra unidad perdida, el desamparo
que es ser hombres, la gloria que es ser hombres
y compartir el pan, el sol, la muerte,
el olvidado asombro de estar vivos. (SB:271; OP1:227)

(the rotting masks / which separate each human being from other humans, / each human being from himself, / collapse / for one gigantic moment and we glimpse / our lost unity, the helplessness / of being human, the glory of being human / and of sharing bread, sun, death, / the forgotten amazement of being alive.)

It is significant that the pronominal subject now is 'we.' The couple is no longer the objective 'los dos'; the 'yo' clearly identifies with and is involved in the act of union, which through its revolutionary nature is a world-changing act of combat:

amar es combatir, si dos se besan
el mundo cambia, encarnan los deseos,
el pensamiento encarna, brotan alas
en las espaldas del esclavo, el mundo
es real y tangible, el vino es vino,
el pan vuelve a saber, el agua es agua,
amar es combatir, es abrir puertas,
dejar de ser fantasma con un número
a perpetua cadena condenado
por un amo sin rostro;
                                        el mundo cambia
si dos se miran y se reconocen,
amar es desnudarse de los nombres. (SB:271; OP1:227)

(love is combat, if two kiss / the world is changed, desires become flesh, / thought becomes flesh, wings sprout / from the shoulders of the slave, the world / is real and tangible, wine is wine, / bread tastes like bread again, water is water, / to love is to fight, to open doors, / to cease to be a ghost with a number / condemned to life in prison / by a faceless owner; / the world changes / if two look at each other and recognize each other, / to love is to strip off all our names.)

Love is a liberating force, opening doors and prisons, freeing us from the names and numbers which are the shackles of our existence. The love story of Héloïse and Abélard is evoked momentarily, as an example of defeat in his giving in to conformity, despite her sacrifice of love in concealing their marriage and her willingness to live the dishonour of an apparently illicit relationship. It is better to live in crime, delirious and suicidal passion, to be punished publicly for one's transgressions, than to submit to the daily yoke of the succession of empty hours imprisoning us, the conversion of time into money and the other forms of abstract refuse of our society. An alternative, more difficult option is to separate ourselves from the world through the pure light of sainthood and thus accede to the central Being beyond all names, whom we call God:

el mundo se despoja de sus máscaras
y en su centro, vibrante transparencia,
lo que llamamos Dios, el ser sin nombre,
se contempla en la nada, el ser sin rostro

emerge de sí mismo, sol de soles,
plenitud de presencias y de nombres. (SB:272; OP1:228)

(the world rids itself of its masks / and in its centre, the vibrant transparent being, / we call God, the being without name, / beholds himself in the void, the being without a face / emerges from himself, sun of suns, / fullness of presences and names.)

The 'yo' continues his march through time, but accompanied now by the 'tú,' a human 'tú' who walks beside the 'yo' and talks and laughs. Yet the cosmic and natural images through which she is depicted (tree, river, grain, squirrel, birds, sea spray, star) suggest that the goddess is incarnate in her. And nature herself is liberated and reintegrated in the flow of 'total time':

tiempo total donde no pasa nada
sino su propio transcurrir dichoso. (SB:273; OP1:229)

(total time where nothing happens / except its own blissful passage)

Fein detects in this second half of the poem a change to an outward movement, away from the introspection which, in his reading, characterizes the first half: 'In the second half, the direction of the poet's experience is outward rather than inward. Here the experience of love is dominant, and it is not "yo" but "tú y yo" that is the essence. Love is the mystical approach to life in this half, and becomes its goal, so that the tone, contrasting with the first half, is optimistic' (1986, p. 33). One should not take this scheme in an absolute sense, since there are certainly moments of despair in the second half of the poem, as there moments of great elation in the first half, and to divide the poem into two contrary movements would not do justice to its complex rhythm of psychological ebb and flow (of both thought and emotion). Nevertheless, the division of the poem into two parts, suggested by the 'dateline' of 'Madrid, 1937,' is perhaps a useful organizational principle for thematic interpretation. In the second half, the 'yo' clearly discovers the world-transforming power of human contact and solidarity. Rather than a separate 'tú' and 'yo,' we now see the pronouns intertwined, so to speak, in 'nosotros.' It is the theme of humanity which distinguishes the second half of the poem. Two people are sufficient, for example, to turn the remote, unconscious human memory of a paradisiacal, Edenic state into reality, in a liberation of body and soul beyond names and events in an idyllic realm where time is perceived in its simple essence as a continuous happy flow:

el mundo cambia
si dos, vertiginosos y enlazados,
caen sobre la yerba: el cielo baja,
los árboles ascienden, el espacio
sólo es luz y silencio, sólo espacio
abierto para el águila del ojo,
pasa la blanca tribu de las nubes,
rompe amarras el cuerpo, zarpa el alma,
perdemos nuestros nombres y flotamos
a la deriva entre el azul y el verde,
tiempo total donde no pasa nada
sino su propio transcurrir dichoso. (SB:273; OP1:228–9)

(the world changes / if two, vertiginously intertwined, / fall down together on the grass: the heavens descend, / the trees ascend, space / is just light and silence, just space / open to the eagle of the eye, / the white tribe of clouds flows past, / the body breaks its bonds, the soul sails forth, / we lose our names and float / drifting between blue and green, / total time where nothing happens / except its own blissful passage.)

This assurance of the 'yo' that love has world-transforming significance, which he repeats several times, now gives way to a critical review of human history, beginning with a number of premonitions of ill-fate and mortality exemplified in a number of classic, representative personages ranging from Cain and Abel to Cassandra, Brutus, Montezuma, and Robespierre. In the span from pre-history to history, time works out a tragic pattern in which the fate of humankind seems determined by the stars. There follows a list of the famous assassinations of modern history: Lincoln, Trotsky, Madero. The blood sacrifice that kept the wheel of history turning is seen as a vicious circle of treachery and murder, presided over by the personae of criminal, saint, prophet, and executioner:

los carajos, los ayes, los silencios
del criminal, el santo, el pobre diablo,
cementerios de frases y de anécdotas
que los perros retóricos escarban,
...

y la boca de espuma del profeta
y su grito y el grito del verdugo
y el grito de la víctima. (SB:274; OP1:230)

(the cursing, the laments, the silence / of the criminal, the saint, the poor devil, / cemeteries of sentences and anecdotes / that the dogs of rhetoric scratch through ... /and the frothing mouth of the prophet / and his cry and the cry of the executioner / and the cry of the victim.)

The earlier images of a fertile world transformed by love, filled with the green and blue colours of water and air are now replaced by a world possessed by fire, a fire which is perhaps both an expression of violence, in view of the foregoing stanza, and the elemental fire of the sun god, the principle of the activity of the mind and spirit. Intense mental and spiritual activity, as we know from Jung's work on dream analysis, is typically symbolized by fire and often heralds moments of important psychological growth or transformation.

The 'yo' continues in a philosophical vein, posing questions of conscience: how to respond to the cry of Christ on the afternoon of Good Friday, as He yields His spirit? How to respond to the cries of humankind, and its silences, pregnant with meaning? How to view the progress of time? Has its progress simply been in vain? The 'yo' concludes, in the deepest episode of despair of the poem, that there is no progress or redemption and that time is inexorable because the clock cannot be turned back. The dead lie fixed in their unrepeatable death, like statues of themselves, and the living, changing 'tú' is immobilized in a mask of stone by a 'phantom king.'[24] We all are condemned to alienation, to a life which does not really belong to us. This leads the 'yo' to ask when life ever did truly belong to us, when we ever really were ourselves.

This line of questioning leads the 'yo' to his second important discovery in the second half of the poem: we may call it the principle of the other. Since life does not belong to us, but rather we collectively *are* life, our life is for others and for the others that we are. We are most truly ourselves when we become others. Only through others does the individual totally exist, and there is no 'yo,' but rather a 'nosotros':

la vida no es de nadie, todos somos
la vida – pan de sol para los otros,
los otros todos que nosotros somos – ,
soy otro cuando soy, los actos míos

son más míos si son también de todos,
para que pueda ser he de ser otro,
salir de mí, buscarme entre los otros,
los otros que no son si yo no existo,
los otros que me dan plena existencia,
no soy, no hay yo, siempre somos nosotros. (SB:275; OP1:231)

(life belongs to nobody, we all / are life – bread of life for others, / all the others that we are – / I am another when I am, my acts / are more my acts if they are also everybody's acts, / for me to be I must be another, / move out of myself, find myself in others, / the others who are not if I do not exist, / the others who make my existence complete, / I am not, there is no me, it is always we who are.)

The search for true existence now leads the 'yo' to cry out to his anima figures 'Eloísa, Perséfona, María' – lover/transgressor, goddess, and saint – for a visual revelation of his true identity, his true face. Unconscious psychological processes have filtered through to rare heights of conscious awareness. The true face of the ego is a collective face, both singular in its collectivity and plural in its various individualities, the human face of humble individuals (baker, driver, sailor, any old Peter and Paul), yet also the face of nature, of tree, cloud, and stream (the elements of earth, air, and water). This is the culminating moment of consciousness in the poem, the definitive moment of psychological birth: 'despiértame, ya nazco' (awaken me, I am being born) (SB:276; OP1:231).

The nascent 'yo' next invokes the dual goddess we have already identified in earlier passages: the goddess of death and life, darkness and the dawn. He pleads for rebirth of his ashes and scattered bones,[25] and asks her to open her hand so that rebirth can take place and dawn appear. In the dialectic process already noted, he asks for both insight for himself and the ability to cross the bridge of inspiration to 'the other shore':

adonde yo soy tú somos nosotros
al reino de los pronombres enlazados. (SB:277; OP1:232)

(where I am you are we / in the realm of pronouns intertwined.)

He asks her also to open her being, to learn to be, to possess a face to look and to be looked at:

puerta del ser: abre tu ser, despierta,
aprende a ser también, labra tu cara,
trabaja tus facciones, ten un rostro
para mirar mi rostro y que te mire. (SB:277; OP1:232)

(portal of being: open your being, awaken, / learn also to be, fashion your face, / mould your features, have a face / to look at and be looked at by my face.)

He asks her to be consciousness, an individual being with a distinct face, instead of the spring welling up from unconsciousness, where all faces melt together in the nameless, faceless, ineffable being:

rostro de mar, de pan, de roca y fuente,
manantial que disuelve nuestros rostros
en el rostro sin nombre, el ser sin rostro,
indecible presencia de presencias. (SB:277; OP1:232)

(face of sea, of bread, of rock and fountain, / spring dissolving our faces / in the nameless face, the being without a face, / unspeakable presence of presences.)

The 'yo' wishes to progress further, beyond this, his supreme revelation, but he cannot. As individuals we are creatures of instants, and each instant, however immense in its fullness, is only an instant followed by another, and yet another:

quiero seguir, ir más allá, y no puedo:
se despeñó el instante en otro y otro. (SB:277; OP1:233)

(I would continue, go further, but I cannot: / this moment crashed down into another and another.)

The individual, personal chronology contained in the discourse of the 'yo' will be followed by other personal chronologies. The circle will begin again, with the possibility of either mechanical repetition or transcendence. In the moment of supreme revelation, the imprisoned blood of the 'yo' begins to flow again, he awakens from dreams of stone and sees doors and walls crumble as the sun's bright rays stream in through his forehead:

dormí sueños de piedra que no sueña
y al cabo de los años como piedras
oí cantar mi sangre encarcelada,
con un rumor de luz el mar cantaba,
una a una cedían las murallas,
todas las puertas se desmoronaban
y el sol entraba a saco por mi frente,
despegaba mis párpados cerrados,
desprendía mi ser de su envoltura,
me arrancaba de mí, me separaba
de mi bruto dormir siglos de piedra. (SB:277; OP1:233)

(I slept the undreaming sleep of stone / and after years like stones / I heard my captive blood singing, / the sea was singing with a sound of light, / one by one the walls gave way, / all the doors were falling down / and the sun came streaming through my forehead, / loosening my closed eyelids, / releasing my being from its shroud, / tearing me from myself, freeing me / from my brutish sleep of centuries of stone.)

The 'yo' here becomes one with the 'tú,' becomes the god in the centre of the stone. The conscious ego awakens the statue and becomes the other, the statue, the stone face he awakens. Human being and godhead, male and female, mother and son[26] are conjoined, and the process of separation and individuation will then begin all over again, in another cycle. Time has come full circle and, like a river, it surges, ebbs, meanders, forever arriving:

un caminar de río que se curva,
avanza, retrocede, da un rodeo
y llega siempre. (SB:277; OP1:233)

(a flowing of river in a curve, / forwards, backwards, in a meander / constantly arriving.)

Conclusion

Having described in some degree of detail the process of *Piedra de sol* and the major elements of the mythical background, we may now listen again to Jung and briefly describe the entirely parallel process of alchemy. The alchemists sought to produce, in a process which was both physical and spiritual (a psychical projection, in Jungian terms), the separation, purification and fusion of chemical elements leading to the creation of the 'philosopher's stone' (*lapis*) or 'philosopher's or king's son' (*filius philosophorum / filius regis*). The alchemists described the process in a variety of ways, with a richness of mythical and symbolical allusions couched in a spiritual language in a way which is disconcerting for the modern mind. Nicolas Barnaud gives the following version: 'Bury, they say, each thing in the grave of the other. For when Sulphur, Sal and Acqua, or Sol, Luna and Mercurius, are in our material, they must be extracted, conjoined, buried and mortified, and turned into ashes. Thus it comes to pass that the nest of the birds becomes their grave, and conversely, the birds absorb the nest and unite themselves firmly with it. This comes to pass, I say, that soul, spirit and body, man and woman, active and passive, in one and the same subject, when placed in the vessel, heated with their own fire and sustained by the outward magistery of the art, may in due time escape [to freedom]' (1602; quoted in Jung 1963, p. 65). Jung develops the idea of the union of elements in the process, in the following manner:

> In alchemy the fire purifies, but it also melts the opposites into a unity. He who ascends unites the powers of Above and Below and shows his full power when he returns again to earth. By this is to be understood the production on the one hand of the panacea or Medicina Catholica, and on the other, of a living being with a human form, the *filius philosophorum*, who is often depicted as a youth or hermaphrodite or child. He is a parallel of the Gnostic Anthropos, but he also appears as an Anthroparion, a kind of goblin, a familiar who stands by the adept in his work and helps the physician to heal. This being ascends and descends and unites Below with Above, gaining a new power which carries its effect over into everyday life. (1963, pp. 227–8)

Jung is careful to dissociate the *filius philosophorum* from a Christ-figure, since this son is a son of prime matter in Nature, not of God directly: 'Above all, the prima materia is the mother of the lapis, the filius philosophorum' (p. 18), and again: 'The alchemical drama leads from below upwards, from the darkness of earth to the winged, spiritual *filius macrocosmi* and to the *lux moderna;* the Christian drama, on the other hand, represents the descent of the Kingdom of Heaven to earth. One has the impression of a mirror-world, as if the God-man coming down from above – as in the Gnostic legend – were reflected in the dark waters of Physis' (p. 103). Jung is at pains to make this dissociation precisely because alchemists so often couched their descriptions in Christian language. They did not do so as an attempt to gain new insight into Christian dogma, however, but rather for their descriptions, as a source of analogy, much like the mirror images that the poetic 'yo' seeks through words at the beginning of *Piedra de sol.*

Though the Christian tradition was the obvious symbolical source of reference to many alchemists, myth and legend also afforded models. Paracelsus, in *De vita longa* (1562) refers, as a backdrop, to the Melusina legend, of which we have already made several mentions. It is instructive to read Dorn's 1583 paraphrase of Paracelsus's text:

> [Paracelsus] says that Melusina, i.e. the vision appearing in the mind, departs from her nymphididic nature into another transmutation, in which she will remain if only that difficult Adech, that is, the inner man, permit, that is approve: who brings about both, that is, death and life of the Scaiolae,[27] that is the mental operations. The first times, that is, the beginnings, of these he permits, that is, favours; but at the end he changes himself, namely because of the distractions that intervene and impede, so that the things begun, that is, the operations, do not obtain their effect. From which [Paracelsus] concludes that the supermonic [inspired from above] figments, that is, enigmatical speculations, in the Cyphanta [distilling vessel], open a window, that is, the understanding, by means of the operations of separation or preparation, but in order to become fixed, that is, brought to an end, they have to oppose the acts of Melusina, that is divers visions and observations, which of whatever kind they may be, he says, we dismiss. Returning to the nymphididic realm, in order that [she] may be conceived in our minds, and that in this way we may attain to the year Aniadin,[28] that is, to a long life by imagination, we take the characters of Venus, that is, the shield and buckler of love, to resist manfully the obstacles that confront us, for love overcomes all difficulties; which characters, even if you know yourselves one with others you have nevertheless put to little use. And thus Paracelsus brings to an end those things which he treated of in the earlier passages, that we may safely obtain that life over which Aniadus, that is, the efficacity of things, dominates and reigns, and which endures for ever with him, namely the heavenly Aniadus, in whom we are present without end: this and other mysteries are in no need of nothing whatever. (Jung, 1967, pp. 174–5)

Though we have spoken of the Melusina legend as a 'model,' this is perhaps the wrong term, since Paracelsus's account is not analytic 'scientific' thought in anything approaching a modern sense and serves to illustrate just how intimately the physical processes of nature are conceived as bound up with the personal objective of the alchemist, higher self-development and understanding, and thereby with 'mysteries' of the internal spiritual processes of humankind. The major topic of the quoted passage is, in fact, the birth and development of the inner invisible Anthropos, and the parallels with the process and the Venusian cycle of *Piedra de sol* will be apparent. Nowadays we may speak of the process in terms of psychic evolution and projection. Melusina, in the last analysis, is the perfect representation of the anima in the process of the development of the masculine self. She is the water nymph who takes on human form as a beautiful, alluring woman in the male mind, but who must return to her watery existence – that is, disappear as an initially helpful, but ultimately deceptive vision – if she is to serve her anima function as mediator between the conscious and unconscious mind.

Piedra de sol is also a poetic description of the birth of ego-consciousness. This process, both in alchemy and in cosmogonies around the world, is visualized in archetypal terms as the birth of light out of darkness. Jung describes it in the following fashion:

> All the worlds that have ever existed before man were physically there. But they were a nameless happening, not a definite actuality, for there did not exist that minimal concentration of the psychic factor, which was also present, to speak the word that outweighed the whole of Creation: that is the world, and this is I! That was the first morning of the world, the first sunrise after the primeval darkness, when that inchoately conscious complex, the ego, the son of the darkness, knowingly sundered subject and object, and thus precipitated the world and itself into definite existence, giving it and itself a voice and a name. The refulgent body of the sun is the ego and its field of consciousness – *Sol et euis umbra*: light without and darkness within. In the source of light there is darkness enough for any amount of projections, for the ego grows out of the darkness of the psyche. (1963, p. 108)

The psychical significance of the Aztec myth of creation, the myth of the four suns, will by now be apparent. Four previous worlds are perfected in the fifth sun, the quintessential full consciousness. And a better description of the essence of Paz's poetic version of the myth than the passage from Jung that we have just quoted can hardly be imagined. In the movement through four suns to the single sun face at the centre of the mandala, 'nameless happening' receives a name and becomes 'definite actuality.' The light of the conscious ego is born, as its sun rises in the 'first morning of the world.' As the sunlight inevitably projects a shadow, so the ego, recently plucked from the unconscious, bears with it its own darkness. The primeval struggle between light and darkness, good and evil, the seen and the unseen begins, the fight between the archangel and the dragon which Jung sees as the first step in the process of integration of a fuller self, the self which transcends the solitude of the ego, existing through the other and through whom the other can exist. The self born of 'the combat of love,' as Paz describes it ('amar es combatir,' SB:271; OP1:227).

No doubt, the symbolical coincidences that we have traced between *Piedra de sol* and alchemy will to many appear far-fetched. It is that fact which makes them remarkable. They do not, of course, give the slightest indication that Paz was either referring to them or had any interest in them per se. Therein lies their significance. They belong to the universal regions of the human mind, where Quetzalcoatl and Coatlicue, Venus (love) and Mercury (transformation) meet, in the circle of death, redemption, and rebirth. They are, like the symbols of *Piedra de sol*, neither European, Asian, nor Mexican, but the symbols of humankind.

Phase Three

Blanco: Mandala and the Ritual of Meaning

Introduction

In the third phase of his creative development, Octavio Paz fully assimilates concepts from eastern philosophy, religion, and culture into the aesthetic of his poetry. *Blanco* in this respect represents a moment of maturity and fruition.[1] Our dialogue between Paz and Jung will continue now along two separate lines: on the one hand, the current of archetypal images connected with the mandala in dream symbolism and in this poem; on the other, the resonances between the two with respect to the concept of relativism which Paz draws from Madhyamika Buddhism and which, for Jung, informs the development of his depth psychology.

Blanco is described by Enrico Mario Santí as 'el poema más ambicioso que ha creado Octavio Paz,' and in many ways it is his most complex poem; 'ambitious' and 'complex' as Santí points out, are the adjectives used by Paz himself to describe this work (1997, p. 301). Santí's documentation of the successive editions and critical summary of the major influences and Paz's personal commentaries on it constitute a skilful and comprehensive introduction to the poem.[2] As Santí points out, this text, which is really a set of multiple poems in one, evolves under the triple influence of structuralism (that of Jakobson but also particularly that of Lévi-Strauss, about whom Paz is writing a book at this time; see 1967b), of Tantric Buddhism and the continuation of his own reflections on otherness and erotic love, as set forth in a pivotal essay for his poetics, 'Los signos en rotación.'[3] Paz is conscious in the mid-1960s of the need for a new poetry to respond to the challenges of a modern technological age, in which the 'image of the world ... rooted in the unconscious structure of society'[4] has largely disappeared, leaving us with 'a repertory of signs possessing temporal and variable meanings', a 'blank space, the same for all mankind.'[5] From such reflections derive not only the concept of the open or indeterminate work commented on by Santí,[6] but the physical concept of the poem as a blank space or surface on which signs are inscribed and whose very substance is time:

> The surface on which the signs are inscribed, whether they be phonetic characters or ideograms, is the equivalent, or rather the manifestation of time which simultaneously sustains and consumes the verbal architecture which constitutes the poem. That architecture, since it is made of sound, is also temporal, with the result that the poem literally constructs and deconstructs itself in our presence. What sustains the poem is the very thing that devours it: the substance of which it is made is time. The page and the Chinese writing roll are both mobile because they are metaphors of time: space in movement which, as if it were time, constantly denies itself and thereby reproduces itself. Temporalization of the page: the written sign does not rest in a fixed space, as does a painting, but rather on a surface which, since it is an image of time, *passes by*.[7]

As the above quotation shows, time is the notion underlying Paz's dynamic view of the poem as the space where poetry happens, and the relevance of the comparison of the poem to a sacred text of ideograms and 'Tantric emblems' is immediately apparent. As Paz states in the prefatory remarks or 'Advertencia' in *Blanco*, the text is 'Something like the stationary journey to which we are invited by a roll of tantric paintings and emblems: if we unroll it, there unfolds before our eyes a ritual, a kind of procession or pilgrimage ... where to? Space flows, engenders a text, lets it vanish – it passes by as if it were time.'[8] Two features of the passages just quoted stand out in particular. On the one hand, there is the expression of paradox based on analogy: the poem is a 'stationary journey' which 'passes by *as if it were* time.' On the other, there is an underlying comparison of poetry with the visual arts. Poetic signs have a visual presence like 'ideograms,' 'paintings,' 'emblems,' and the poetic text as a whole is a 'verbal architecture.' We will return shortly to the architectural concept of the whole.

As noted in previous chapters, the expression of paradox concerns the symbolic act. The symbol, as we have seen, concerns the irrational, intuitive side of language, and it is also the constructor of poetic – that is, human meaning. As Paz says, 'man is a communicator of symbols.'[9]

What is new for Paz in the 1960s is the realization that the symbol stands in an 'as if' relationship to the linguistic sign. The founder of structuralist linguistics, Ferdinand de Saussure, contended that the sign was arbitrary, that its content or *signifié* was abstract, fixed, and virtual (1916, pt 1, chaps 1 and 2). The natural complement to the theory of the sign is to be found in the work of another great structuralist, Émile Benvéniste: in order for it to be invested with meaning, the sign is enunciated by a speaker, who through his message constructs the 'other,' the hearer.[10] The sign-symbol association would seem to be, in part, a reflection of Paz's consciousness of the splitting of the word, in modern western culture, into rational and irrational halves. It is also (in the spirit of Eco, Cortázar, and John Cage) the realization of the 'open work' in the most radical sense: the work of art does not exist outside its (re)enunciation by the reader, and the artist is simply its first enunciator. Poetic communion depends on truly collective construction.

The struggle of the poet documented by Paz in his surrealist period of the 1940s and 1950s now becomes the struggle for sense of Everyman, the Reader. This struggle is built upon another paradox: that of permanence and impermanence. The world has lost all permanence because the images, the symbols of that world, have been broken. Meaning has been replaced by power.[11] The symbol then becomes the responsibility of the individual, its presence belongs to the individual act of enunciation. Its reality is its endless repetition in one individual enunciation after another, its temporal flow. Yet Paz describes this reality not as time itself, but as a figuration of time, an image recurring 'as if' it were time. Form and meaning, sign and symbol are fundamentally distinct, yet held together in a tension of energy.

In the context of these reflections on sign and symbol, the idea of a poetic architecture of wholeness acquires a particular significance. As a verbal edifice, the poetic text is quite literally a centre of energy, held up in empty air, so to speak, by its own sound and fury, yet signifying nothing outside itself. In its very materiality, though, it is a presence, a body inviting contemplation, an inner journey towards the centre of the self. The analogy here with the gnostic journey of tantrism is complete: on the one hand, the close identification of the body with spirit, which for the western mind is a difficult concept to embrace; on the other, the view of the body as a tree of life, through which kundalini or life energy ascends through six centres, or chakras (*cakras* in Sanskrit). This is a journey of passion, a ritual of ecstasy. As the epigraph to *Blanco* from the Hevajra tantra states: 'By passion the world is bound, by passion too it is released.'

Just as Cortázar gives indications for reading *Rayuela*, so Paz explains, in his prefatory 'Advertencia,' the different ways in which this poem, composed over two months in 1966 in Delhi, can be interpreted. First, it can be read in its entirety as a single poem, unfolding it in a single scroll. Secondly, the centre column can be read as a single poem on the passage of the word from silence to silence, from the blank page to white space, after passing through four colour states: yellow, red, green, and blue. The left-hand column can be read as four moments of a poem corresponding to the traditional four elements of nature. The right-hand column comprises another poem reflecting four mental faculties: sensation, perception, imagination, and understanding.[12] Four additional, different poems can be composed by joining the left- and right-hand parts. Finally, the centre column can be read as a series of six poems, and the right- and left-hand columns as eight separate poems. The multiples of four here, elements of the process described by Jung as 'squaring the circle,' constructing the mandala as an archetype of wholeness or totality, are clearly evident in the poem's architecture.

The structure of *Blanco* can also be compared to a body, particularly the multiple-limbed body of a tantric image, through which the kundalini flows. For a full account of the articulation of the poem, encompassing its intertextual sources, the Hevajra tantra and Mallarmé's poem 'Un coup de dés,' the chakras and channels of energy between them, rasana and lalana, and even a diagram of the poem (see Ulacia 1999, pp. 297–332). Here, we concentrate on the chakras and certain acoustic images, visual forms, and colours associated with them as mandalas, which are not mentioned by Ulacia.

Indra Sinha describes the meditative process of tantric yoga and the flow of psychic energy through the body in the following manner (1995, pp. 104–6). The *muladhara* or root chakra, the first psychic centre of the body, is situated at the base of the spinal column. The *muladhara* is related to the element of earth. Associated with it is a 'yantra,' or geometrical figure for meditation, of a lotus with four crimson petals bearing four golden letters as seed mantras. Halfway up towards the navel is the *svadisthana* chakra, with a yantra of six vermilion petals and associated with water and the seed-syllable 'la.' At the level of the navel is the *manipura* chakra, with a ten-petalled lotus and associated with fire and the seed-syllable 'ram.' Located in the area of the heart is the *anahata* chakra, with a twelve-petalled lotus and associated with air and the seed-syllable 'yam.' The *visuddha* chakra is at the base of the throat, with a lotus of sixteen petals and a white circle representing the element of ether. Its seed-syllable is 'yam.' The sixth *ajna* chakra is situated between the eyebrows and has a lotus with two white petals bearing the golden letters 'ham' and 'ksham.'[13] In the centre of the lotus is the sacred syllable 'Om'; it is a mental centre, a site of far-seeing, brightly illuminated by the light of the soul. Transcending the body is a seventh chakra, the *sahasrara* chakra, the abode of the Supreme Deity, conjoined as Siva-Sakti, masculine and feminine, home of the realized kundalini, whose knowledge means liberation from the bonds of *samsara*, from rebirth, in the final freedom of death.

This journey of gnosis is an implicitly sacred, ritual comparison with the process of the modern reader of the poem reading through it and creating meaning. Both are ritual acts in that their meaning may be endlessly repeated, each time the same, yet each time different. We will return later to the symbols which the chakras and the poem have in common. Suffice it to say here that these tantric centres of energy are closely associated with language in the form of mantras.

One might think that, with such points of reference, Paz might compare the structure of the poem(s) to the geometrical figures for meditation known as yantras. Yet in his 'Advertencia' he chooses to describe the poem as a 'mandala,' the symbol of cosmic and individual centredness and wholeness: 'This temporal arrangement which is the form followed by the poem in its course, its discourse, is matched by a corresponding spatial one: the different parts of which the poem is made up are laid out like the areas, colours, symbols and figures of a mandala.'[14] While some yantras are indeed figures of the universe and are mandalas, Paz's choice of descriptive term refers us beyond tantrism to the universal, primeval, archetypal image, which we have already encountered in *Piedra de sol*. The point can be proved in Jungian terms. As we know, Jung established the relationship between eastern mandalas and symbols occurring in dreams of individuals in the west who have no knowledge of eastern thought. It does not surprise us, then, to find that the colours of Paz's poem are exactly those which recur in the dreams commented on by Jung in *Psychology and Alchemy*. The description of Dream 23 runs thus: 'In the square space. The dreamer is sitting opposite the unknown woman whose portrait he is supposed to be drawing. What he draws, however, is not a face but three-leaved clovers or distorted crosses in four different colours: red, yellow, green and blue' (1953a, p. 164). And in Dream 39, it is a bear, image of the *prima materia*, whose eyes glow in the four colours: 'The dreamer is falling into the abyss. At the bottom there is a bear whose eyes gleam alternately in four colours: red, yellow, green and blue. Actually it has four eyes that change into four lights. The bear disappears and the dreamer goes through a long dark tunnel. Light is shimmering at the far end. A treasure is there, and on top of it the ring with the diamond. It is said that this ring will lead him on a long journey to the east' (p. 187). Here the synthesis of the four colours into the white light of the diamond (symbolizing the *lapis*, according to Jung's commentary) which is set in the circular form of the ring is quite evident. The motifs of the ring, the journey to the east, and the white light of the diamond like that of a guiding star are as classical as the biblical story of the magi. In *Alchemical Studies*, Jung reproduces a number of illustrations of mandalas from his personal collection, one of which expresses this same synthesis, which also underlies the organization of Paz's mandala poem, more completely. Jung's description runs as follows: 'In the centre, the white light, shining in the firmament; in the first circle, protoplasmic life-seeds; in the second, rotating cosmic principles which contain the four primary colours; in the third and fourth, creative forces working inward and outward. At the cardinal points, the masculine and feminine souls, both again divided into light and dark' (1967, plate A6). If we take into account that Paz's mandala depicts a universe of language, that 'life-seeds' in that context are gestating words, and that the 'rotating cosmic principles' are 'signos en rotación,' this is a more accurate characterization of *Blanco* that any Tantric parallel could ever give us. Among the various meanings of the polysemic title of the poem, this is the primary one: 'blanco', the white light at the centre, the white centre of the circular target, akin in some ways to the sunlight which 'breaks through the centuries of stone' in *Piedra de sol.* Paz's mandala is quite classic and universal in its form.

The colour symbolism of the mandala pervades not only the religious symbolism of the east, but also that of the west. Jung's main commentary on mandala colours concerns, in fact, the Christian symbolism, partially since this is the major referential context for alchemy, but also because in the chromatic system of the Trinity one colour, blue, is missing. The symbolism can be clarified from an episode from the already-quoted fourteenth-century work by Guillaume de Digulleville, the *Pélerinage de l'âme.* In a vision of Paradise, Guillaume questions his guiding angel about the nature of the Trinity and receives the following explanation: 'The angel answers, "Now, there are three principal colours, namely green, red, and gold. These three colours are seen united in divers works of watered silk and in the feathers of many birds, such as the peacock. The almighty King who puts three colours in one, cannot he also make one substance to be three?" Gold, the royal colour, is attributed to

God the Father; red to God the Son, because he shed his blood; and to the Holy Ghost green, "la couleur qui verdoye et qui réconforte"' (1953a, pp. 212–13). It can hardly escape our notice, though, that the missing fourth colour, blue, is the colour associated with the Virgin Mary. Jung, throughout his work, makes repeated reference to the psychological significance of the Assumption of the Virgin, which we need not go into here. Suffice it to say that there are psychological reasons for transforming the Trinity into a quaternity that have nothing to do with religious dogma.

The colour white, in this interpretation, is an expression of fullness, of synthesis, of complete being. In the tantric parallel we briefly described above, it also symbolizes transcendence: the white circle of the ethereal element, the white lotus flower, and the illuminating light of the spirit which characterize the higher chakras. At the same time, we have seen that Paz in his 'Advertencia' describes his title as emptiness, silence, the white page, the nothingness existing before and after the poem. *Blanco* as word and title is thus also a conscious expression of polarities, founded upon a reflection derived from Mahayana Buddhism. That Paz's frame of reference at the time is eastern religious thought is clear from a letter written in 1967 to Díez Canedo, documented by Santí: 'Another later letter (9 February 1967) to Diez-Canedo ... reveals that the author first thought of giving it the title *Sunyata*, 'which means void or emptiness and which in Mahayana Buddhism also means reality – reality of realities: Samsara is equivalent to Nirvana, reality to unreality, madness to wisdom.' But after also discarding this first title, he chooses *Blanco*: 'it means the same as *Sunyata* – even in the sense that it is a state which is by definition unattainable, this target we never reach.'[15] Santí goes on to explain how 'sunyata' represents an evolution in the eastern influences on Paz's thought since his initial encounter with Buddhism in the 1950s. The idea of emptiness or impermanence belongs to 'a combinatorial theory of the world and the ego which prefigures contemporary logic,' and it is the understanding of this notion, rather than the triumph of the poetic paradox over rationalistic thought, which represents true illumination:

> It is precisely the realization that Buddhism is based 'on a combinatorial theory of the world and the ego which prefigures contemporary logic,' as the same passage of *Claude Lévi-Strauss* goes on to say, that is Paz's decisive step towards comprehending this oriental thought; which is, it will constitute the step of transition from his first encounter with Buddhism in the

> 1950s to that of a decade later. A transition from Zen to Madhyamika Buddhism and, particularly, its development by Nagarjuna, its most famous 'logician' (150–250 AD). While the highest aspiration of the first trend is sudden illumination (*satori* or *koan*), the second posits by contrast something much more radical: what reveals the essential character of the relationship is nothing less than the void, impermanence (*Sunyata*). True knowledge, then, will no longer consist in the triumph of paradox over logic, or even its subsequent illumination, but in the void.[16]

The concept is disconcerting to the western mind because it is misunderstood. Emptiness and impermanence are simply expressions of a relativistic view of existence, that things do not exist independently of each other: 'By the term *void* Madhyamika Buddhism (and Nagarjuna in particular) did not mean non-existence (which is how we in the west would interpret the concept), but another truth: that everything is relative. Indeed, at least in its first stage Madhyamika thought is relativist, since it conceives of things as lacking what Buddhism calls *svabhava*, their "own being." Since nothing has independent or eternal substance, things, since they are images of dreams or illusions, neither exist substantially nor cease to exist absolutely.'[17]

Relativism applied to language gives rise to a dialectic of language, as Paz notes towards the end of *Claude Lévi-Strauss o el nuevo festín de Esopo.* Words in relation are a binding together of differences, of otherness, not a resolution of contradiction: 'The essence of the word is the relationship, and thus it is that it becomes the figure, the momentary incarnation of everything that is relative. Every word gives rise to another that contradicts it, every word is the relationship between a negation and an affirmation. Relationship means binding together of otherness, not a resolution of contradictions. For that reason language is the dialectical realm which constantly destroys itself and is reborn only to die again. Language is dialectic, operation, communication.'[18]

Santí cogently refers Paz's eastern view of relativism back to the idea of the 'open work' and his explanatory note included with the first edition of *Blanco,* which speaks of the possibility of combining two contradictory elements: extension and intensity, concentration and succession, what happens here and what happens there.[19] As Santí observes, the idea goes beyond mere precepts of literary theory. The 'open work' for Paz belongs to a metaphysic, negating determinism, and elevating the freedom of chance and accident, which are forms of 'otherness,' to a structural aesthetic principle:

> In the first place, we should recognize that the observation goes further than a simple detail of literary criticism, or what a Spanish critic, in his commentary on the poetics of the open work, once called 'the hour of the reader.' Rather, it is a metaphysical viewpoint which recognizes the freedom of reading and challenges the reader of the open work to assume that liberty in all its dimensions. 'In India – Paz observes in another passage of *Corriente alterna* – negation, no less subtle than its western conception though applied to different things, is at the service of indeterminacy; its function is to open the doors of the unconditioned for us' (p. 141). That is, the indeterminacy of the open work signals, in the final analysis, the indeterminacy of life: the 'unconditioned' component which we are wont to call Chance, Luck, Accident, Adventure, or Destiny, forms of *otherness*. As a game of writing, the open work confronts the reader with his own liberty.[20]

This is also an aesthetic, though Santí does not say so at this juncture, which harks back to the source of the second epigraph of *Blanco*, Mallarmé's 'Un coup de dés.'

Commentary on the poem

The outline we have briefly traced of the aesthetic operative in *Blanco* will serve to underline the difference between the mandala of this poem and that of *Piedra de sol*. In an oft-quoted passage of her book on the mythic dimension in Paz's poetry, Frances Chiles points out that '"Piedra de sol" is the perfect example of what Frye calls the pictorial or emblem poem, in which "the pictorial shape of the subject is suggested in the shape of the lines of the poem"' (1987, p. 103). The mandala referred to in *Piedra de sol* is the Aztec calendar stone, and the poem seeks to reflect the shape of the stone in its own circular structure. The movement and rhythm of the poem set in motion the contemplation of the referent, and the poem refers to the meditations of the 'yo' subject and the interaction of his consciousness with the unconscious. *Blanco* is an even more 'pictorial' poem in that it is pure emblem in itself, not a reflection of another emblem. In the case of *Blanco* the mandala is the poem itself, and the poem is its own referent. The contemplation and the movement are provided by the reader in his/her construction of one or many poetic texts between the initial and final white space (silence).

This self-referential autonomy sheds a rather different light on the expression of archetypal images in *Blanco* than we have seen in previous poems of Paz. The poem is an assemblage of universal images, many of which we have seen in *Piedra de sol* and earlier poems: the elements of water, wind, earth, the tree, the female other, and so on. The ultimate meaning of those images, though, relates not to Paz or the poetic subject in his texts, but to the individual reader. There is only one truly archetypal image in *Blanco* and that is the mandala which is the poem itself. It is as much an icon as a symbol, a space where the tensions of the meanings invested in it by the reader will play out his story (there is no history in *Blanco* in a referential sense). The rest is simply words, symbolic as much in their materiality as in the associations the reader will choose to give them. They spread out over the space of the verse, as shown in the first page of the poem:

el comienzo
                    el cimiento
la simiente
                    latente
la palabra en la punta de la lengua
inaudita   inaudible
                    impar
grávida   nula
                    sin edad
la enterrada con los ojos abiertos
inocente   promiscua
                    la palabra
sin nombre   sin habla. (SB:485)

(the beginning / the foundation / the seed / latent / the word on the tip of the tongue / unheard unhearable / unequal / pregnant void / without age / the woman buried with her eyes open / innocent promiscuous / the word / without name without speech.)

Or they flow together as in successive pages. Sometimes the letters pull apart, leaving blank spaces between (as, in fact, they do on the first page quoted above, though we have not shown it as such), while at other times they follow a more normal letter spacing. The pages vary in font, the poems in colour, and words and verses come together or pull apart in an alternating motion. It is not difficult to attribute a (cosmic) sexual dimension to this alternating flow if, as reader, one chooses to do so.

Apart from the tensions created by the spacing of the words, visual patterns emerge: the five adjectives which immediately follow 'la palabra en la punta de la lengua' are organized as four points around a centre, a mini-mandala and a true yantra. The last two, 'grávida' and 'nula,' as antonyms express the principle of emptiness and fullness that we have discussed above. The pattern is repeated in the last three verses of the page, where 'inocente' and 'promiscua' stand in antonymic relation. Or do they? Only in a culturally specific sense, in fact, since Paz would like to defend the idea that innocence and promiscuity are natural allies, whose alliance is opposed to our world dominated by the 'non-body' sign, as he explains at the end of *Conjunciones y disyunciones*, written some two years after *Blanco* and published in 1969:

> I have already stated my belief that modern time, linear time, homologous with the notions of progress and history, always looking to the future, the time of the sign of *non-body*, determined to subjugate nature and repress instinct, the time of sublimation, aggression, and self-mutilation, our time, is coming to an end ... The time which is returning, if we are in fact experiencing a return of earlier times, a thorough turn-around, will be neither future nor past but a present ... Carnal time, mortal time: *the present is not unattainable, the present is not forbidden territory* ... our incredulous eyes will witness the awakening and return to our abject world of that bodily and spiritual reality that we call 'loving presence.' Then love will cease to be the isolated experience of an individual or a couple, an exception or a scandal.[21]

Love, when our present age ends, will cease to be an isolated act and regain the innocence of presence, and 'love' and 'presence,' he says in the closing words of the book, hold the secret of our resurrection. On the verbal plane, there is an invitation to the reader to break down his or her conventional distinctions, the barriers between terms that can have no intercourse with each other because they have opposite canonical or conventional meanings; in short, Paz launches an invitation to the adventure and rebellion of language.

Another tension apparent in *Blanco* is between written and spoken language, between words as graphic and phonic forms. The first page, again, sets in motion a field of phonic associations, which in turn propose morphemic ones. The yantra fuses with the mantra in the repetition of the syllable 'cim(iento) – sim(iente)' recurring later as the word 'sin (edad / nombre / habla)' or the 'ie' diphthong at the beginning. On the third page, a similar process is at work in the sibilants, liquids, and nasals of 'Silencio/sello/centelleo.' This is the process of gestation of the word, before it is word, before it emerges into consciousness. It is both the potentiality of language emerging from silence and the alchemy of discourse free of its conscious trappings, as Kugler would have it, which is language free to establish the phonetic associations which destroy the barriers created by discrete, univocal meaning. As Kugler affirms: 'An archetypal study of sound-images has as its task a psychological understanding of the relation between the multiple meanings that have become attached to similar phonetic patterns, to the 'polysemy' (multiple meanings) in language' (1982, p. 89). Archetypal psychologists have stressed the relativism both of Jung's conception of archetype in the collective unconscious and of the whole process of interpretation of meaning in the dream. Patricia Berry (1974), for instance, has argued for the relative and multiple interpretations of the dream image, and on the topic of how to determine whether an interpretation of a dream is right or wrong, James Hillman writes: 'Wrongness now means singleness. The constructs of right and wrong imply an either/or world, not the polysemous, polyvalent one of dreams and images. When we realize the inherent multiplicity of meaning in the image itself, we cannot force the dream into any single truth' (1978, p. 156). Concerning the relativism of Jung's own view, Kugler notes: 'in 1912–13 Jung abandoned the causal-mechanistic view of the psyche based upon libido and adopted instead an energic view in which psychic energy was seen as relational. The move from libido to psychic energy, from a theory based on the primacy of substances to one founded on the primacy of relations, allowed Jung to adopt a structural approach to the collective layer of the personality. Jung viewed the personal unconscious as an ineffable refuge of personal memories and individual particularities, complexes filled with the substance of a unique history, and the collective unconscious was thought to be an empty and purely formal set of structural relations called archetypes' (1982, p. 68). Kugler backs up his view by quoting Jung's comparison of archetypes to the structure of a crystal:

> Again and again I encounter the mistaken notion that an archetype is determined in regard to its content ... The representations themselves are not inherited, only the forms ... With regard to the definiteness of the form, our comparison with the crystal is illuminating inasmuch as the axial system determines only the stereometric structure but not the concrete form of the individual crystal. This may be either large or small, and it may vary endlessly by reason of the different size of its planes or by the growing

> together of two crystals. The only thing that remains constant is the axial system, or rather, the invariable geometric proportions underlying it. The same is true of the archetype. In principle, it can be named and has an invariable nucleus of meaning – but always only in principle, never as regards its concrete manifestation. (Jung 1959a, p. 79)

In *Blanco* the axial principle is the word, which becomes verse, poem, then poem of poems. The word is not so much a unit as a microcosm, the same tension-filled space as the space of each individual poem and the space which all the poems occupy in the macro-poem of the whole text. Each word and each image points towards the mandala, or becomes the mandala. What constitutes the mandala is space, and the energy which fills the space between words is imaged in a positive/negative polarity growing out of the repetitions of words and becoming an organizing principle throughout the poem. The process is most evident in the sixth and last (central-column) section of the poem: 'apariciones/desapariciones,' 'real/irreal,' 'sí/no' (the latter described as 'dos sílabas enamoradas'). This polarity is, we might say, a constructive principle of the body of the poem, as well as a technological metaphor for the mental energy jumping like an electrical charge from one term to another. Joining the list of polarities by virtue of association are 'blanca y negra' and 'habla/silencio.' As we have already tried to illustrate in our commentary on the antonyms on page one, these polarities represent not a structure of pre-established or canonical meaning, but a process of discovery and critical reflection, an invitation to re-examine traditional oppositions between words. Yet at the same time it is a door open to the primitive adventure of sound and to the unconscious patterns and associations liberated thereby.

We stated above that the only archetypal image in *Blanco* was the mandala as the poem itself. We can expand now upon that initial simplification after quoting the clarifications by Kugler and Jung concerning the formal, geometric nature of the archetype. There are a host of potential symbols in *Blanco* which we can easily recognize not only as universal symbols from nature (for instance, river, tree) and from major cultural and religious traditions (the Christian images of 'Pan Grial Ascua,' for example), but also as the classical personal symbols which appear throughout Paz's poetry. Some of these could be interpreted in an archetypal sense: for instance the first sub-poem in red (the right column), dealing with sensation, could be seen as an allegory of the alchemy of the spirit: the 'leona' and 'leones' as regal animals evoke the archetypal figures of 'Rex' and 'Regina,' and the circle of flame evokes fiery sulphur. Alternatively, we might view the anima in the circle of flame as the soul in the centre of the fire of the heart, following Paracelsus's conception (Jung 1963, p. 46). Nevertheless, the point is that these symbols actually acquire archetypal significance only in relation to the personal unconscious of a subject, the poet/reader (the only access to the collective unconscious being, in the final instance, through the personal unconscious), just as the Christian significance of figures of 'Pan Grial Ascua' may or may not be actualized by the reader. Unless it passes through the personal perception and understanding of the individual reader, *Blanco* contains no symbols at all, only dead words. However, the pointer to potential archetypal significance of the local images of the poem is perceived through their formal resemblance to the central archetype, the mandala. This is the only pictorial or emblematic representation of archetype in the poem; the others, which are potentially there, are expressed through language. The association with the archetype is clear in the recurring circular images in the poem. For instance, in the example just quoted from the poem on sensation, the anima in the centre of the circle is clearly a figuration of the mandala:

llama rodeada de leones
leona en el circo de las llamas
ánima entre las sensaciones. (SB:487)

(flame surrounded by lions / lioness in the circus of the flames / anima among sensations.)

The association of the anima with the idea of wholeness has been explained on several occasions by Jung (see, for example, 1963, pp. 307, 356ff.).

In the second poem in red, on perception, the classic image of the river is depicted circularly:

rueda el río seminal de los mundos
el ojo que lo mira es otro río. (SB:489)

(the seed river of the worlds turns / the eye beholding it is another river.)

And in the fifth central-column section of the poem, five senses are portrayed as circling in a ring around a precious stone, a centre of introspection, which through its colour of amethyst is possibly reminiscent of the sacred lotus flower of tantric association:

> Gira el anillo beodo,
> giran los cinco sentidos
> alrededor de la amatista
> ensimismada. (SB:491)

(The drunk ring revolves, / the five senses revolve / around the self-absorbed amethyst.)

In the first lines of the sixth and last central-column poem, body and spirit are united in a sexual image as the centre of the world:

> En el centro
> del mundo del cuerpo del espíritu
> la grieta el resplandor. (SB:493)

(In the centre / of the world of the body of the spirit / the crevice the glow.)

These images of ring, sexual union, union of body and spirit are clearly mandala images of a maturing human psyche. As Neumann explains: 'But to the maturing psyche, slowly integrating itself under the sign of the hermaphrodite, the world, too, assumes the appearance of the hermaphroditic ring of existence, within which a human centre takes shape, be it the individual who comes to self-realization between the inner and outer worlds, or humanity itself. For humanity as a whole and the single individual have the same task, namely, to realize themselves as a unity' (1954, p. 417). This process of maturation of the self in the second half of life will culminate for Paz in *Carta de creencia*, under the sign of the human couple, which we have identified as the fifth and final phase of his creative development.

Another circular mandala image in *Blanco* is that of the flower, if we see it in sacred terms as the tantric lotus (centre of concentration of energy) or the golden flower of Taoism.[22] It would seem natural to read this image in a tantric sense, given the associations with mind and language of the words which surround it, as well as the potential religious association of 'cáliz.' It seems clear that it is an inner, mental flower, gold in colour and formed by the fiery language of the spirit:

En la palma de una mano
ficticia,
        flor
ni vista ni pensada:
                    oída,
aparece
        amarillo
cáliz de consonantes y vocales
incendiadas. (end of second central-column poem; SB:486)

(In the palm of a fictitious / hand / a flower / unseen unconceived: / heard, / appears / yellow / chalice of consonants and vowels / on fire.)

The combination of potential western and eastern religious and symbolic associations in the poem that we have briefly alluded to is, in fact, just one facet of its essentially eclectic nature. *Blanco*, in the final analysis, is not simply a verbal entity. It is a complex of interrelated semiotic systems, each with its own meaning potential: sound, image, colour, elements, psychic modes, numbers. In the terms of modern semiotics, we would call it a multimodal text.[23] With respect to number symbolism, the number six, of tantric association, combines eclectically with the quaternary four-eight combinations of other dimensions of mandala symbolism. Paz's objective is to create a total meaning construction environment.

Conclusion

To summarize and conclude, we have attempted to trace the philosophy, semiotics, and aesthetic behind Paz's richest, most novel and most explicit configuration of a poetic mandala. None of our observations, however, really explains the essential fascination of the mandala form for Octavio Paz, not even his intense interest in eastern philosophy and culture during the 1960s. To attempt an explanation we must leave the last word to Carl Jung.

Jung's essential discovery in his exploration of the psychological significance of the mandala is that, rather than simply being a form, it functions as a centre of energies, a structure of tensions between yoked opposites, a place where meaning happens as signs revolve around a common centre. This dynamic conception pervades his every description of of the mandala and explains its therapeutic psychological effects. He points out that 'as a rule a mandala occurs in conditions of psychic dissociation or disorientation' (1959a, p. 387) and goes on to show how 'a circular image of this kind compensates the disorder and confusion of the psychic state – namely, through the construction of a central point to which everything is related, or by a concentric arrangement of the disordered multiplicity and of contradictory and irreconcilable elements' (p. 388). Hence the therapeutic qualities of the mandala, since 'this is evidently an attempt at self-healing on the part of Nature, which does not spring from conscious reflection but from an instinctive impulse' (ibid.).

If we look closely at what Jung characterizes as 'the formal elements of mandala symbolism,' namely: 'circular, spherical, or egg-shaped formation'; the circle elaborated into a flower'; 'a centre expressed by a sun, star or cross, usually with four, eight or twelve rays'; 'the circles, spheres and cruciform figures are often represented in rotation'; 'a snake coiled about a centre,' 'squaring of the circle,' 'castle, city and courtyard' motifs, 'eye' (1959a, p. 361), we see that beneath every apparent form or symbol lies a process. In her explication of *Blanco* as mandala, Román Odio (2000) refers to four of Jung's elements as motifs of otherness in the poem: the (nascent and unfolding) flower, the squaring of the circle, the rotation of signs, and the (empty) centre. All are both form and process, and in that respect she clearly shows the consonance of Paz's poetic design with Jungian thought. As both form and process, *Blanco,* in the final analysis, is an image of the universe, and its reader 'reinvents the body of the universe,' in Ulacia's words (1999, p. 349). It is also an image of the union of ego and the various voices of the self, the richest of all Paz's poetic spaces, where poetry, true meaning, can happen.

Phase Four

Vuelta, Nocturno de San Ildefonso, and *Pasado en claro*: The Circular Journey and Return to the Source

Introduction

In Jungian psychology, the human life cycle is clearly divided into two halves: the first concerned with the birth of ego consciousness, the second with the birth of the self. On various occasions Jung refers to the first and second halves of life, but it is Neumann who sums up the matter succinctly, relating the two halves respectively to the motifs of dragon fight and night sea journey: 'The dragon fight of the first period begins with the encounter with the unconscious and ends with the heroic birth of the ego. The night sea journey of the second period begins with the encounter with the world and ends with the heroic birth of the self. This last phase of conscious development is no longer archetypal, i.e. collectively conditioned, but it is individual. Archetypal materials may have to be assimilated as well, but they are assimilated consciously and by an individual who attains self-experience through his unique and idiosyncratic union with the transpersonal worlds within and without' (1954, pp. 415–16).

Phases One and Two of Paz's creative development evolved under the common sign of a struggle or fight (even love being defined in these terms: 'amar es combatir'). After the turning point and creative watershed of *Blanco,* though, Phase Four is marked by the sign of the journey, not a sea journey (since, like Gilberto Owen, another Mexican poet of the *Contemporáneos* group,[1] Paz is a mariner cast up on dry land), but certainly a nocturnal journey. Or, more accurately, it is a progress towards the nocturnal journey of self-discovery. For Paz the journey starts as a uniquely circular journey, a journey whose goal is now a return to the source. The return to the source continues to be a search for the centre, as Paz continues to work with the mandala image of unity, order, and integration of the self. These late mandalas of phase four, however, will be much more personal and individual than *Piedra de sol* and *Blanco,* since they are built upon references to Paz's personal present and past in Mexico and are less structured by archetypal images, just as the quotation from Neumann above would lead us to predict.

Paz's poetry of the 1970s contains a number of poems having in common the motif of circularity, the longest three of which will be the material analysed in this chapter. From circular forms in concrete poems such as 'Anotaciones/Rotaciones,' which includes the 'Adivinanza en forma de octágono,' building on themes and geometries first proposed in *Blanco,* to the poem entitled 'Poema circulatorio (para la desorientación general),' produced for the 1973 exhibition on surrealist art in the Museum of Modern Art in New York, the poems published in the book *Vuelta* show a veritable fascination with the circle. However, the three longer poems we are concerned with, *Vuelta, Nocturno de San Ildefonso,* and *Pasado en claro,* propose not merely circularity but, as we have noted, a circular journey. Their interest, in this respect, is that they represent a new phase of psychic development. They can be seen as three stages of the quest for the self, progressing from circumambulation to the purposeful night journey of self-discovery. *Pasado en claro* (1974) can be seen as a summation of the preceding two poems (just as *Piedra de sol* is a summation of the poems which precede it in *La estación violenta*). Even though *Blanco* constitutes a model for virtually all of Paz's poetic production as a mature poet, these poems also represent a break with *Blanco.* They represent a continuation but also a new beginning, in that they are a return to specific and concrete personal content.

The poetic return in the three poems corresponds also to a homecoming, Paz's physical return to Mexico. The term for return in Spanish, 'vuelta,' is, of course, polysemous: it also means a 'turn,' a 'stroll,' and a (possibly infructuous) circular journey. Its connotations vary from casual diversion to frustration. These are the various meanings and connotations which are active in the first poem, *Vuelta.*

Jung has characterized the circular journey as an aspect of the progress of the unconscious: 'The way to the goal seems chaotic and interminable at first, and only gradually do the signs increase that it is leading anywhere. The way is not straight but appears to go around in circles. More accurate knowledge has proved it to go in spirals: the dream-motifs always return after certain intervals to definite forms, whose characteristic is to define a centre. And as a matter of fact the whole process revolves about a central point or some arrangement round a centre, which may in certain circumstances appear even in the initial dreams. As manifestations of unconscious processes the dreams rotate or circumambulate round the centre, drawing closer to it as the amplifications increase in distinctness and in scope' (1953a, p. 28). He goes on to compare the spiral unconscious process to the symbol of the plant and the tree, connoting growth: 'We might draw a parallel between such spiral courses and the processes of growth in plants; in fact the plant motif (tree, flower, etc.) frequently recurs in these dreams and fantasies and is also spontaneously drawn or painted. In alchemy the tree is the symbol of Hermetic philosophy' (pp. 28–9).

Vuelta begins, like *Blanco*, with sounds, but they are not the sounds of syllables and phonemes of the poet's words; they are the voices and whistles of workmen: the carpenter, the iceman, other typical tradesmen of the streets of Mexico City. The poet is plunged into the midst of down-to-earth humdrum reality as never before in his poetry. He is conscious of walking back in time towards 'lo que dejé / o me dejó' (what I left / or what left me behind) and time is hung out to dry like sheets on the rooftop *tendederos* so typical of the Mexican capital. He is back in the place of his birth and infancy, Mixcoac.

The return to the source is simultaneously the possibility of a new beginning, fraught with danger. Looking forward through memory, the poetic subject, the 'yo,' the traveller, sees he is on the edge of a precipice, and he feels as if he were on a balcony suspended over the void:

Memoria
inminencia de precipicio
balcón
sobre el vacío (SB:598; OP2:35)

(Memory / imminence of the precipice / balcony / over the void.)

The 'yo,' immersed in a new labyrinth of solitude, back in the place which he left, or which left him years ago, walks aimlessly in meaninglessness, oppressed by his urban surroundings, but insubstantial, without a presence:

Camino sin avanzar
estoy rodeado de ciudad
Me falta aire
me falta cuerpo. (SB:598; OP2:35)

(I walk without advancing / I am surrounded by city / I lack air / I lack a body.)

He misses the stone and the grass (in terms of archetypal significance, a centre, an anchor, a sense of the self, on the one hand, and creative growth on the other). He has no guide into the unconscious because the guiding light of the anima disappears: 'se apaga el ánima.' The poet reflects on the images of death which pervade the poem, but even death has no meaning. The funereal pomp of funeral homes lives side by side with prostitution in the red light district. The language is heavily ironical: the very conventionality of the term 'pompas fúnebres' robs it of sense, and the 'putas' become in a hilarious and picturesque euphemism 'pilares de la noche vana' ('pillars of the vain night'). The nocturnal images in the poem are mere figments of a futile passage of time, and have nothing to do with the night voyage that the poet will later be invited to take.

Though the wasteland depicted by Paz smacks of the disenchanted urban realism of a Carlos Fuentes novel (if there is any influence here, it runs both ways, since *Vuelta* is quite explicitly a source for Fuentes's quaternion of short stories entitled *Agua quemada*), the poem is certainly not about social realism. In tone and intent, Paz's *Vuelta* has a much greater affinity with Eliot's *The Waste Land*. Yet in Paz, unlike Fuentes and Eliot, the demons of the mind are never far way. The 'leprous images' of which the poem is full grow quite literally from nightmares:

Germinación de pesadillas
infestación de imágenes leprosas
en el vientre los sesos los pulmones
en el sexo del templo y del colegio. (SB:598; OP2:35)

(Germination of nightmares / infestation of leprous images / in the belly the brain the lungs / in the sex of the temple and the school.)

The description of urban society and its institutions dominated by avarice and the powerful and meaningless peso-dollar sign '$' is nightmarish in the extreme. Though at first sight the description seems pictorial, encompassing the vision of both a Posada and the Mexican muralist painters in their moments of virulent social protest, there is an energy in the scene, which suggests, in Jungian terms, the menacing chthonic aspect of the unconscious through the presence of dangerous and bloodthirsty animals. Rarely have the Aztec words of Mexican Spanish been used with their colloquial overtones to such great effect in describing animal nature:[2]

En esquinas y plazas
sobre anchos zócalos de lugares comunes
los Padres de la Iglesia cívica
conclave taciturno de Gigantes y Cabezudos
ni águilas ni jaguares
los licenciados zopilotes
los tapachiches
alas de tinta mandíbulas de sierra
los coyotes ventrílocuos
traficantes de sombra
los beneméritos
el cacomixtle ladrón de gallinas
el monumento al Cascabel y a su víbora
los altares al máuser y al machete
el mausoleo del caimán con charreteras
esculpida retórica de frases de cemento. (SB:599; OP2:36)

(On street corners and in squares / on broad boulevards of commonplaces / the Fathers of the Civic Church / silent conclave of Giants and Bigheads / not eagles or jaguars / the legal vultures / the locusts / with inky wings and saw-sharp jaws / the ventriloquist coyote middlemen / shadow traffickers / the distinguished members of society / the hen thief cacomistle / the monument to the Rattlesnake and his viper / the altars to the mauser and the machete / the mausoleum of the shoulder-padded uniformed alligator / sculpted rhetoric of sentences of stone)

Jung speaks of such animal incarnations of the unconscious in the process of 'circumambulatio': 'But if the life-mass is to be transformed a *circumambulatio* is necessary, i.e., exclusive concentration on the centre, the place of creative change. During this process one is "bitten" by animals; in other words, we have to expose ourselves to the animal impulses of the unconscious without identifying with them and without "running away"; for flight from the unconscious would defeat the purpose of the whole proceeding' (1953a, p. 145). This is not to say that the animal figures in *Vuelta* are manifestations of the personal unconscious in exactly the way that they happen to be in the dream Jung is referring to here.

Paz's description has an undeniable dimension of conscious social message. Yet there is no doubt that this society of predators represents a dark obstacle to the expression and realization of the self and to the attainment of happiness, not only for the poetic subject, but for humankind in general. (Even in his most personal poems, Paz never ceases to be a social poet.) The menacing entrapment that these figures represent is summed up in a short half-verse (all the verses of the poem are half-verses, broken verses): 'Estamos rodeados' ('We are surrounded').

The adversary is the enemy of meaning and of language: signs, words, and languages are broken:

Noticias de ayer
                más remotas
que una tablilla cuneiforme hecha pedazos
Escrituras hendidas
                    lenguajes en añicos
se quebraron los signos
                        atl tlachinolli
               se rompió
                        agua quemada. (SB:600–1; OP2:37)

(Yesterday's news / more remote / than a cuneiform tablet broken in pieces / Split writing / shattered languages / the signs were broken / it broke atl tlachinolli / burnt water.)

The mention here of the classic Aztec oxymoron 'atl tlachinolli,' which, as Paz explains in his notes to the poem, in Aztec society signified the harmonious dialectic of opposing forces, is particularly important. Unlike this Aztec metaphor for the cosmic harmony of union of opposites, signs in the modern capitalist world are broken apart, emptied of meaning. In the present context, 'atl tlachinolli' makes an obvious surface reference to the barrenness of a world without the element of fecundity: water, either spiritual or physical. Nevertheless, we should not forget the deeper reference to water as the element of the unconscious. The words suggest that the unconscious has 'dried up' and burnt out because the futile daily routine of conscious, or rather half-conscious, life is entirely separated from it. 'Atl tlachinolli' as a paradox is also an expression of a cyclical transformation: birth, destruction, rebirth, and so on. Yet the poet can only declare his impotence in the face of this challenge:

No hay centro
plaza de congregación y consagración
no hay eje
dispersión de los años
desbandada de los horizontes. (SB:601; OP2:37)

(There is no centre / square for congregation and consecration / there is no core / dispersion of years / scattering of horizons.)

There is no centre, no sacred gathering place, time and space scatter and fragment, and the poet realizes that he is back where he started, with only a pointless question on his lips:

He vuelto adonde empecé
¿Gané o perdí? (SB:601; OP2:37)

(I am back where I started / Did I win or lose?)

The only conclusion is that both winning and losing mean the same, and thus is revealed to the poetic subject an essential truth: that he must lose himself to find himself. Suddenly he discovers the way for the journey into himself, towards the centre, here depicted as 'the little square' (that of the Mixcoac of his infancy?):

Camino hacia mí mismo
hacia la plazuela
El espacio está adentro
no es un *edén subvertido.* (SB:601; OP2:38)

(I walk towards myself / towards the little square / Space is inside of me / it is not a *subverted Eden.*)

This is not the nostalgia of a López Velarde, bemoaning the past and lost innocence in the 'subverted Eden' of the present, but the sudden pulse of time itself and a 'fluttering of presences,' imagined presence taking flight. The voices of water and of the union of darkness and light ('luz y sombra') are heard and seen for a moment among the leaves of the ash trees. They shine for a second, flow, and then are lost. The poet is left to continue, without progressing, on his circular journey, since the present, and presence, are unattainable. There is, however, a subtle change in the last verses of the poem: the switch to a plural subject, from 'I' to 'we.' Is it motivated by a sense, on the part of the poet, that his predicament is that of the human condition in general, or is it an emergence from isolation? The incipient realization, on the part of the poet, that he is not alone?

Nocturno de San Ildefonso

The topic of our second poem or second stage, *Nocturno de San Ildefonso,* is the poet's journey into the spiritual night of this world to which he is returning. San Ildefonso, significantly situated in the heart of the old downtown or centre core of Mexico City, the 'centro histórico' as it is now called, is the street where Paz attended the Escuela Nacional Preparatoria, on the site of the old Jesuit college of San Ildefonso. This is the place where, as an adolescent, Paz first came to grips with the intellectual issues of society, art, history, and politics, where his initiation into the adult world began. The mature poet will now repeat this process of initiation, which is a descent into the void:

Caigo
interminablemente sobre ese vacio. (SB:630; OP2:63)

(I fall / interminably upon this void)

The theme of the night journey is an age-old motif in the literature of fiction and the imagination, and Jung examines the specific variant of the night sea journey, describing it as 'a descent into the dark world of the unconscious ... the perilous adventure of the night sea journey ... whose end aim is the restoration of life, resurrection, and the triumph over death' (1953a, p. 329). It is also the 'nekyia,' the descent into Hades, or the land of the dead (p. 53n).

As we have noted, there is no perilous sea journey in Paz's poetry, but the first part of *Vuelta* might be seen in a certain sense as a perilous descent into a land of the dead. The same process of descent into a dead world can be observed even more distinctly in the second poem, *Nocturno de San Ildefonso.* In any case, what we have afterwards is a restoration of the self through a resurrection of language, a reinvigoration of the broken signs to which *Vuelta* alludes. The ensuing personal odyssey culminates in a personal statement or letter of belief: *Carta de creencia,* Paz's last long poem. Hence the importance of the return to the personal past, the recreation in writing and in the imagination of life experiences from childhood on.

Nocturno de San Ildefonso begins in a framework of imagination, created by signs. The present night (of perceived reality) is recreated as another night (the internal night, the night of imagination), where signs explode into consciousness as if in a firework display:

Signos-semillas:
la noche los dispara,
suben,
estallan allá arriba,
se precipitan,
ya quemados,
en un cono de sombra,
reaparecen,
lumbres divagantes,
racimos de silabas,
incendios giratorios,
se dispersan, otra vez añicos.
La ciudad los inventa y los anula. (SB:629–30; OP2:62)

(Seed-signs: / shooting from the night, / they rise, / explode up high, / hurtle down, / burnt out already, / in a cone of shadow, / they reappear, / wandering lights, / bunches of syllables, / spinning fires, / they scatter, / into little bits again. / The city invents them and nullifies them.)

The context is not literal reference to the external world, but rather the journey into a world of personal significance, where through mental and spiritual activity, meaning is reborn. The invitation to the voyage is felt as a momentous moment breaking out of time, a journey into the mouth of a tunnel with, perhaps, one's true self waiting at the other end:

Estoy a la entrada de un túnel.
Estas frases perforan el tiempo.
Tal vez yo soy ese que espera al final del tunel.
Hablo con los ojos cerrados. (SB:630; OP2:63)

(I am at the entrance to a tunnel. / These sentences bore through time. / Perhaps I am the one waiting at the end of the tunnel. / I speak with closed eyes.)

The page is alive with moving signs, like an anthill, and nervously the poet throws himself into the mental abyss, in what seems to him a never-ending fall without movement:

> Caigo
> interminablemente sobre ese vacio.
> Caigo sin caer.
> Tengo las manos frías,
> los pies frios
> – pero los alfabetos arden, arden.
> El espacio
> se hace y se deshace. (SB:630; OP2:63)

(I fall / interminably upon this void. / I fall without falling. / My hands are cold, / my feet are cold / – but the alphabets burn, burn. / Space / forms and disperses.)

The poet feels night, the unconscious, touching his forehead and his thoughts and dares to stand and ask '¿Qué quiere?' What does it want?

In the second section of the poem, the poet has entered into a world of the dead, the world of his own past, dated furtively as 'México, hacia 1931.' Empty streets and 'one-eyed' lights create a phantasmagorical and unreal world inhabited by fleeting spectres: the ghost of a dog, a flight of sparrows and a band of newspaper boys sheltering in a 'nest' made of the newspapers they did not sell, the flash of the skirt of a prostitute, who is a figure of death or a dead woman ('la mort ou la morte'). The blackness of the night is palpable, almost solid: 'un cielo de hollín.' The red walls of San Ildefonso, black in the night, evoke a city of another time, when these streets were canals and the houses were silver and white, like a moon which has fallen into the lake. The challenge, as the poet now sees, is to reconstruct not just his personal story but the history of Mexico, 'our history,' to rebuild a city from the 'petrified gardens of symbols' in the buildings all around, from the 'callada nación de las piedras,' a 'nation' of stones. These are specific stones of personal significance, Mexican stones and a Mexican city, but we cannot forget their archetypal nature as symbols which we have already encountered in phase one, in our commentary on *Libertad bajo palabra:* the stone as a symbol of the self and the city as an archetype often associated with an anima figure. The associations with whiteness and with the moon, essentially female associations, will be taken up a little further on. The point we wish to emphasize here is the guiding and structuring significance of the city, the fact that 'el viento verbal,' the spirit of words, constructs not castles but cities in the air, spiritual cities which are imaginative geometries, projections connected to reason by a slender thread:

geometrías
suspendidas del hilo de la razón. (SB:633; OP2:65)

(geometries / hanging from the thread of reason.)

The architecture of personal experience becomes, through symbol, the architecture of writing. The letters on the page assume a shape and permanence, like stones.

In the third section of the poem, the mature poet is writing himself as a young idealistic boy: both his past and the page he is writing are a 'caminata nocturna,' the poet observes in an aside. The moral questions of the young Paz and his colleagues growing up and being absorbed into the system are addressed:

Algunos
se convirtieron en secretarios de los secretarios
del Secretario General del Infierno. (SB:634; OP2:67)

(Some / became the secretaries to the assistants / of the General Minister of Hell.)

Mexican Spanish, in one of its supremely bureaucratic words, has managed to synthesize the notions of the underdog and the person of power and influence in a single term. 'Secretario,' whose translation into English would require, at the very least, two terms like 'secretary' ('assistant,' 'aide') and 'minister,' summarizes the whole vertical power structure of the Mexican State. How to avoid the moral error of treason, the error of submission to this power structure? The poet concludes that history itself is the error. The only salvation is in poetry, in the verbal sun stones, the 'stelae' or acts of writing which are monuments to moments of cultural and historical perception. In the words of the poet himself, he has chosen the 'act of words, making them, inhabiting them, giving language eyes.' The reference here to *Piedra de sol* is evident, just as explicit reference is also made, earlier in the poem, to the poetic project of *Blanco*:

Del amarillo al verde al rojo
se desovilla el espiral. (SB:629; OP2:62)

(From yellow to green to red / the spiral unwinds.)

Nocturno de San Ildefonso is one of the most intertextual of Paz's poems, as also is *Pasado en claro.*

In the fourth section, the ideas engendered by the edifice of language disperse and the spectres return, but time remains. As a collective rage and oblivion, it is nonetheless transformed and preserved by memory, and like a collective body it attains concrete existence in language. The poet is back now from the nocturnal outside world, inside his room. The window, lit by the commercial world of flashing neon lights, behind which real stars are scarcely visible, is suddenly illuminated by an authentic presence: the moon. In earlier epochs the moon was a goddess and now, the poet says, it is a 'claridad errante,' a wandering or travelling light, or a guiding light, clarity for the traveller. The whiteness of the moon and its feminine associations identify here a residual archetypal meaning in the alchemical symbol of Luna. This feminine whiteness is another of the polysemous virtualities of the title of *Blanco,* an aspect which we did not explore in our brief commentary on that poem, but which can be done through the multiple images of erotic love and sexual union in it.

The poet who in his earlier work battled for clarity through language now, in the final section of *Nocturno de San Ildefonso,* finds clarity as a gift at the end of the tunnel of his personal experience. The light into which he emerges at the end of that tunnel is that of the other, the feminine principle. What follows is one of Paz's most beautiful invocations of woman, dedicated to 'mi mujer': she is also moon, she is water, torrent, flow. It was the text he chose to read in December 1997 in what must have been one of his last recorded messages which, too ill to attend in person, he sent to be played at the inauguration of the chair established in his honour at the National University of Mexico.

As dawn breaks, the poet surrenders to the end of his nocturnal journey, his own end, his death, wondering whether death will be an ascent or a descent. He closes his eyes. He awakes, still alive. The room is full of the silver sand of moonlight. The presence of Woman is a 'fuente en la noche': fountain in the night, but also a source. At the end of his journey of return, she is his source and he finds direction and confidence in her safe haven, her soft flow.

Pasado en claro

The third exploration of the circular journey motif is Paz's longest poem of the 1970s, *Pasado en claro.* The title is typically polysemous, referring to both writing and experience: it means both 'the past, seen clearly' and something like 'pasado en limpio,' a clean or final version of an initial draft. It refers, then, both to a process of clarification and to its result: 'pasado' is both noun and participle. For this reason Fein, in his commentary on the poem, concludes, along with other critics, that its meaning 'rests on opposing interpretations' and that the title 'is contradictory' (1986, p. 122). The title expresses a contradiction to the extent that the whole poem expresses or incorporates a paradox, just as the individual image did in his early poems. There is per se nothing particularly new or revolutionary in this. Paz offers us his personal history from the same vantage point as Eliot's 'still point of the turning world' in *The Four Quartets*. What *Pasado en claro* does, as a culmination of the *circumambulatio*, is to define a centre and draw close to it, in the process described by Jung in the quotation cited at the beginning of this chapter. The protagonist of the night journey emerges into clarity, the previously broken words and images are reintegrated into a harmoniously flowing whole, and the return to the place of origin is not a vicious circle, an aimless, meaningless meander, as it was in *Vuelta*, but an ordered synthesis, a coherent summation.

Result and process are, in fact, the same reality seen from different focal points. As the poet states in the final stanza of the poem, 'yo soy mis pasos': 'I am my steps,' my actions are my being, my essence is my transience. The centre and the journey coincide. 'I enter an abandoned patio,' the poet says. It is a protected centre, a walled patio with a tree and a well, an airy place on the other side of which is emptiness:

> Entro en un patio abandonado:
> aparición de un fresno.
> Verdes exclamaciones
> del viento entre las ramas.
> Del otro lado está el vacío. (SB:644; OP2:76)

> (I enter an abandoned patio: / ghost of an ash tree. / Green exclamations / of the wind among the branches. / Beyond it the void.)

The tree as archetype appears in various personal avatars: 'baniano, fresno, higuera.' They are concrete figurations of different moments, different points on the revolving circle of the poet's personal existence.

The poem's structure incorporates two pivotal symbols: the tree and the mirror. Both are classic images for Octavio Paz, recurring throughout his poetry. They are, for instance, prominent in *Piedra de sol*, even if we have not devoted extensive attention to them. As noted at the beginning of the chapter, Jung sees in the tree 'a 'poetic' comparison that draws an apt analogy between the natural growth of the psyche and that of a plant' (1963, p. 349). The alchemists referred to this comparison as the 'philosophical tree,' to which topic the whole final section of Jung's *Alchemical Studies* is devoted. Jung clarifies part of the complex nature of the tree in describing it as both 'opus' (finished work) and 'transformation process': 'In so far as the tree symbolizes the opus and the transformation process "tam ethice quam physice" (both morally and physically), it also signifies the life process in general. Its identity with Mercurius, the *spiritus vegetativus*, confirms this view. Since the opus is a life, death, and rebirth mystery, the tree as well acquires this significance and in addition the quality of wisdom' (p. 338). The tree symbol embodies, then, the 'contradiction' expressed by Fein. It is the same 'árbol bien plantado mas danzante' ('tree firmly planted yet dancing') as we see in the initial/final verses of *Piedra de sol*. By its association with human identity and process, it is also the tree of knowledge: 'from man [= Anthropos] and gnosis is born the tree, which they also call gnosis' writes Irenaeus in the *Adversus haereses* (pp. 338–9). The same principles can be illustrated through the close association between the stone and tree symbols. The stone, as a symbol of the (centred) self, is also a vegetative process. Jung explains this through quotations from the alchemists: 'Similarly the "Consilium coniugii," commenting on Senior, says: "Thus the stone is perfected of and in itself. For it is the tree whose branches, leaves, flowers, and fruits come from it and through it and for it, and it is itself whole or the whole [*tota vel totum*] and nothing else." Hence the tree is identical with the stone and, like it, a symbol of wholeness' (pp. 319–20).

Another association with the tree and the stone patio and well in the poem is the house, the house of Paz's infancy, which is also a broader, collective space, as we can see from its association with the square and its various trees (not one only) and the squat church:

Casa grande,
encallada en un tiempo

azolvado. La plaza, los árboles enormes
donde anidaba el sol, la iglesia enana. (SB:651; OP2:82)

(Large house, / stranded in the sediment of time. / The square, the enormous trees / where the sun nested, the squat church.)

The mirror, as the other pivotal image of the poem, underlines the mutual reflections between reality and language, between life and literature, between the conscious ego and the unconscious self. In this respect, there is a subtle play of meaning centring around the word 'ojo': this is both the perceiving eye and the 'ojo de agua,' the water source or well, the unconscious depths reflecting the eye/I in a mutual exchange:

por donde sube el agua y baja
mi sombra. (SB:645; OP2:76)

(where the water is drawn up and / my shadow descends)

This mutual exchange is worked out, in the poem, through a constant interplay of light and shadow, the potential of creative harmony glimpsed at the end of *Vuelta*, the union of light and dark or harmonious interaction of the conscious with the unconscious and, in the final instance of vision (the act of seeing), with language. The mental shadows cast against the light of the spirit represent language and are the very topic with which the poem begins:

sin caminar caminan
sobre este ahora, puente
tendido entre una letra y otra. (SB:643; OP2:75)

(They walk without advancing / over this present, bridge / between one letter and another.)

The emergence and growth of language is compared to a plant or tree:

Y la negra marea de las sílabas
cubre el papel y entierra
sus raíces de tinta
en el subsuelo del lenguaje. (SB:643–4; OP2:75)

(And the black tide of syllables / covers the page and buries / its inky roots / in the subsoil of language.)

The ultimate discovery of Paz in this poem is that the coherence of personal history implies its nature as text. Indeed, the individual's very identity depends on his belonging to the vast text of the world. Language, the black marks on the white page, the discrete calligraphies moving over the backdrop of the pure light of the spirit. Both 'animals and things become languages,' says the poet, and through language we are, as microcosm, one with the universe:

a través de nosotros habla consigo mismo
el universo. Somos un fragmento
– pero cabal en su inacabamiento –
de su discurso. (SB:656; OP2:87)

(Through us the universe speaks / to itself. We are a fragment / – but consummate in our incompleteness – / of its discourse.)

The discourse of the universe tells us that it enounces us and tells itself the same. As a harmonious, coherent system it is, by definition, language.

The journey through concrete personal experience begins in the luminous city of Paz's Aztec past, which is presented not only as 'reality' but as representation, a pictorial space in the style of a codex, integrating speech in the form of a horizontal comma, which is also, Paz points out, a solitary piragua rowing across the lake:

Rima feliz de montes y edificios,
se desdobla el paisaje en el abstracto
espejo de la arquitectura.
Apenas dibujada,
suerte de coma horizontal (ᵕ)
entre el cielo y la tierra,
una piragua solitaria. (SB:645; OP2:77)

(Happy rhyme of hills and buildings, / the line of landscape is continued in the abstract / mirror of architecture. / Scarcely traced, / a kind of horizontal comma / between earth and sky, / a solitary dugout canoe.)

Earth and sky meet, then, in a single act of speech. History turns the harmonious vision of the city and the lake into the bloody destruction of Tenochtitlan, the history Paz reads in the books of his grandfather Ireneo's library:

> Los libros del estante son ya brasas
> que el sol atiza con sus manos rojas. (SB:645; OP2:77)

> (The books on the shelf have turned to burning coals / which the sun fans with his red hands.)

The beauty of the lake is eclipsed in the writing of the official versions, but life and the whispers of untold truths still peer like eyes from among the foliage of the letters.

The poet realizes that he does not 'see' through his memory, but through language:

> Un charco es mi memoria.
> Lodoso espejo: ¿dónde estuve?
> Sin piedad y sin cólera mis ojos
> me miran a los ojos
> desde las aguas turbias de ese charco
> que convocan ahora mis palabras.
> no veo con los ojos: las palabras
> son mis ojos. (SB:646; OP2:77)

> (My memory is a pool. / Muddy mirror: where have I been? / My eyes without anger or compassion / look straight up at me / from the murky waters of that pool / which my words now conjure. / I do not see through my eyes: words / are my eyes.)

We live – the poet goes on to elaborate – among names, and what is still nameless has no existence. The pool, here, is a shallow, murky mirror, without the clarity or subterranean depth of the well. It is a mirror of language and, for the poetic subject, a mirror of his own words, reflecting the questions of his own existence:

> Espejo de palabras: ¿dónde estuve?
> Mis palabras me miran desde el charco

de mi memoria. Brillan,
entre enramadas de reflejos
...
las sílabas de agua. (SB:646; OP2:78)

(Mirror of words: where have I been? / My words look at me from the pool / of my memory. They shine / among branches of reflections ... / syllables of water.)

'Seeing' the world means spelling it out, interpreting it as text: 'Ver al mundo es deletrearlo' (SB:646; OP2:78; To see the world is to spell it out).

The answer to the question 'Where have I been?' the poet concludes, is 'where I am,' and through language all past history has access to an eternal present. The memory of the school where Paz studied as a child and his recreation of it in words are the same, yet different, both being and emptiness (= impermanence), both object perceived and the act of perceiving:

– no hay escuela allá dentro,
siempre es el mismo día, la misma noche siempre,
no han inventado el tiempo todavía,
no ha envejecido el sol,
esta nieve es idéntica a la yerba,
siempre y nunca es lo mismo,
nunca ha llovido y llueve siempre,
todo está siendo y nunca ha sido,
pueblo sin nombre de las sensaciones. (SB:648; OP2:80)

(– there is no school there inside, / it is always the same day, the same night always, / they have not invented time yet, / the sun has not grown older, / this snow is identical to the grass, / always and never are the same, / it has never rained and it is raining always, / everything is and never has been, / unnamed village of sensations.)

The journey continues in a fusion of lived and read experiences, both of which are, in the last analysis, forms of intertextuality. Without moving, time rotates in the synthesis of words upon the page:

Giran los años en la plaza,

rueda de Santa Catalina,
y no se mueven. (SB:652; OP2:83)

(The years revolve in the square, / Saint Catherine's wheel, / without moving.)

Then there is the vision and depiction of the house, its labyrinth of 'cuartos' and 'pasillos' where family ghosts and hatreds dwell, the oppressive presences and dubious pressures to 'be somebody' from which the poet must liberate himself in order to be himself. The figures of his mother, his aunt, his father appear briefly and disappear. The dialogue with them is only an imagined one, in dreams. The poet goes on to explain how he has avoided the traps of power, greed, and the comfortable but empty sanctity of institutional religious belief:

No me multiplicaron los espejos
codiciosos que vuelven
cosas los hombres, número las cosas:
ni mando ni ganancia. La santidad tampoco:
el cielo para mí pronto fue un cielo
deshabitado, una hermosura hueca
y adorable. (SB:654; OP2:84–5)

(I was not multiply reflected in the mirrors / of avarice which turn / men into things, things into numbers: / neither power nor gain. Nor sanctity either: / Heaven for me soon became an empty heaven / an empty and adorable beauty.)

His belief is in presence, the discovery of a body, or the bodies of his body, and from the viewpoint of physical sensation, time splits in two and the flesh is made word in the mortal jump into the abyss: 'la carne se hace verbo – y el verbo se despeña' (SB:655; OP2:85; the flesh is made word – and the word falls headlong). Paz discovers death, and rediscovers history, as language:

Y yo en la muerte descubrí al lenguaje.
El universo habla solo
pero los hombres hablan con los hombres:
hay historia. (SB:657; OP2:87)

(And I in death discovered language. / The universe speaks alone / but men speak with men: / history exists.)

History is the sum total of speech acts, of acts of communication, the projection of the face of the other in the blood stain of our Veronica cloth.

Between being and impermanence, the poet discovers a third state of empty plenitude, a discovery made through his exploration of eastern thought. A bodiless god is discovered in the centre of 'nothingness,' of eternal doing and undoing, which is language. The quest to name this deity in the centre of the self is the very reason behind the poet's quest for language, for the deep, unrevealed, unconscious side of language, which the poet half hears in the 'murmullo':

Estoy en donde estuve:
voy detrás del murmullo,
pasos dentro de mí, oídos con los ojos,
el murmullo es mental, yo soy mis pasos,
oigo las voces que yo pienso,
las voces que me piensan al pensarlas.
Soy la sombra que arrojan mis palabras. (SB:660; OP2:90–1)

(I am where I have been: / I follow the murmurs, / steps inside me, heard through my eyes, / the murmurs are in my mind, I am my steps, / I hear the voices that I think, / the voices that think me while I think them. / I am the shadow cast by my words.)

Language is the circle of light and dark in which my presence is the presence of my past, in which my circumambulation will keep repeating the same poem, the same but different each time. The process and the result are one. I am text, and my self is the dark shadow cast by my words.

Phase Five

Carta de creencia: The Human Couple

The title of phase five might be defined in contraposition to that of Jorge Aguilar Mora's book *La divina pareja: Historia y mito en Octavio Paz* (1978) on the essays of Octavio Paz, dealing with a non-divine pair of concepts in an abstract manner. The themes of *Carta de creencia* (1987) are human themes and at their centre is a/the human couple, presented in a divine manner. Perhaps no poem of Paz is more religious than this one, since the human couple is portrayed against a backdrop of references to Adam and Eve and the garden of Eden, and the poem's title presents it as a personal statement of faith, which it certainly is: faith in mankind and the redeeming power of poetry. This is not to say that it is a poem about religious belief in any orthodox or institutional sense. As already noted, Paz's phases of poetic production after *Blanco* are his most intensely personal ones.

In Jungian terms, *Carta de creencia* is the last and simplest of Paz's poetic mandalas, since it requires no complex development of archetypal motifs. It is simply a personal statement of the balanced self, based on the realization of the life principle that everything internal is also external, that what happens up 'above,' at the level of spirit, is reflected in what happens down 'below,' at the level of body. This means that the very basis of completion of the self is the human couple, the union of 'yo'and 'tú,' and likewise that there is no couple without self. The 'tú' is both inside the self and outside, apart from it. There is no contact with the other except through the other that we are. Eve is born of Adam in the biblical account, a process studied by Jung in *Aion* (1959b). In Paz's version she is born from the words of the poet. But as he is also at pains to show, there is no Adam without Eve. The union of Adam and Eve and of the 'above' and the 'below' give us the four points of the quaternity of wholeness in the mandala of *Carta de creencia.* The harmony and balance inherent in the equation can be illustrated by the way the poet now views love: no longer as a struggle, but as a timeless island of light in the midst of darkness (SB:171; OP2:179).

The tree symbol so prominent in this poem and central to the volume to which it belongs, *Árbol adentro,* is the image par excellence of this correspondence of innerness and outerness. The tree is an element of nature, planted by the other, contemplated by the poet, and as we have seen in the circular poems of phase four, an icon closely identified with the poet's childhood. But it is also an interior mental tree, Jung's 'philosophical tree' or 'tree of knowledge,' a concrete symbol of growth of the psyche and of the self: 'In the Ripley "Scrowle," Mercurius appears as a snake in the shape of a Melusina descending from the top of the Philosophical Tree ("tree of knowledge"). The tree stands for the development and phases of the transformation process, and its fruits and flowers signify the consummation of the work' (1959b, p. 235).

The human couple depicted in primeval terms as Adam and Eve is also, in Jungian terms, a representation of a final stage of consummation of the maturity of the self. It is to Neumann that we turn, though, for the most succinct description of the process: 'As in alchemy the initial hermaphroditic state of the *prima materia* is sublimated through successive transformations until it reaches the final, and once more hermaphroditic, state of the philosopher's stone, so the path of individuation leads through successive transformations to a higher synthesis of ego, consciousness and the unconscious. While in the beginning the ego germ lay in the embrace of the hermaphroditic uroboros, at the end the self proves to be the golden core of a sublimated uroboros, combining in itself masculine and feminine, conscious and unconscious elements, a unity in which the ego does not perish but experiences itself, in the self, as the uniting symbol' (1954, pp. 414–15). Here, in the final hermaphroditic stage, we find the deeper meaning of the perfect complementarity of the human couple. This is also the meaning of Neumann's hermaphroditic ring, to which we had occasion to refer in our commentary on the symbols appearing in the text of *Blanco.* Paz's specific contribution to this concept, as also to the corresponding concept of the brotherhood of mankind, is his realization that what unites us as human beings is communication through language, and that language also cements the universe. Cosmic language complements human language: up above, the constellations are always writing the same word, he tells us, while here below we write our mortal names. This realization is part of a consciousness of the power and central importance of language, which has been growing in Paz's mind since *Blanco.* Curiously, this realization is accompanied by a radical simplification of the language used in his poetry: he is reduced to handful of words, which he offers here and now to the beloved in an act of simplest sincerity: 'me quedan estas palabras: con ellas te hablo' (AA:164; OP2:174; I am left with just these words: with them I speak to you).

It is easy, at first sight, to dismiss *Árbol adentro* as less significant than Paz's earlier books of poetry. It contains no poems on the grand scale, no radical or revolutionary, hermetic or esoteric techniques. Indeed, poetic expression seems to have been distilled into simple short verses, touching perhaps in their lyrical quality, but hardly needing a special exegesis. *Carta de creencia* takes up images, topics, and motifs that we have already seen, particularly in *Pasado en claro* and *Blanco.* Yet now they are taken up, in relation not to the personal development of the 'yo,' but to the dialogue of love with a 'tú,' not as figures of poetic discourse or archetypes, but as the poet's personal discourse with his beloved. This is Paz's personal version of the *coniunctio,* so to speak, not as a mystical union or the fusion of the elements in gold, but as an intimate communication on the themes of love, death, and human happiness. *Carta de creencia* bears its title, perhaps, as a statement of belief, but its discourse is musical and idyllic, hence the appropriateness of its subtitle, *Cantata.* Santí, in his commentary on *Blanco,* observes that Paz achieves something in that poem that neither Mallarmé nor tantric Buddhism, his epigraphic sources, do: he composes a love poem. The observation might apply even more fittingly to *Carta de creencia,* which is surely one of Paz's most beautiful love songs, and a swan song as well.

The poem, divided into three sections and a coda (thus structured musically) begins in the indeterminate territory of twilight, the intersection of light and shadow that we have seen in a major part of *Pasado en claro.* The page darkens with the writing of words just as the afternoon darkens and the lines of things are blurred and they lose their substance and reality. The twilight is neither light nor shadow: 'it is time,' the poet tells us. The time vocabulary in this section ('día, noche, tiempo, hora, pausa, tarde') refers to both the time of the world and a personal time. There is perhaps an underlying consciousness of death, of moving towards an end. Reality is withdrawing, but the poet writes and speaks in his here and now. He longs to break out from the solitude of the written word, speaking to his beloved with the same natural elements as do the tree, air, water, and fire, words which are solid, visible, and palpable, like things. Yet things meanwhile transmute to other forms and names, becoming part of the play of language. Language and reality as mutually reflecting mirrors is another theme taken up from *Pasado en claro.*

The poet is left with only a few words. As is the case with most other poems of *Árbol adentro,* their power is apparent only to the reader who is familiar with all of the earlier works of Octavio Paz. The few words left to him synthesize whole poems from before, and *Árbol adentro* is composed of short fragments of concentrated retrospection. At this juncture, though, Paz is concerned not with words or language, but with speech. The verb constantly repeated is 'hablar':

> Me quedan
> estas palabras: con ellas te hablo. (AA:164; OP2:174)

(I am left / with just these words: with them I speak to you.)

Words are the bridges of communication, but they are also prison-houses and traps through which the other cannot hear:

> Las palabras son puentes ...
> También son trampas, jaulas, pozos.
> Yo te hablo: tú no me oyes. (AA:164; OP2:174)

(Words are bridges ... / They are also traps, cages, wells. / I speak to you: you do not hear me.)

Communication between the human 'yo' and 'tú' can only be indirect because words are the projections which intervene. Yet it is possible because the word used by the 'yo' to define the 'tú' can be taken by the 'tú' and used for her own definition. Through such interchange, words both are us and reflect us:

> La mujer que eres
> es la mujer a la que hablo:
> estas palabras son tu espejo,
> eres tú misma y el eco de tu nombre.
> Yo también,
> al hablarte,
> Me vuelvo un murmullo. (AA:164; OP2:174)

(The woman you are / is the woman to whom I speak: / these words are your mirror, / you are yourself and the echo of your name. / I too, / in speaking to you, / become a murmur.)

So profoundly are language and existence intertwined.

Words as bridges and projections imply a space between the beholder and what or whom he beholds. This is the space in which dialogue takes place; it is also aesthetic space, the distance which enables observed reality to be transformed into observed beauty, as, for instance, in the scene of the hills of Meknès, which is the setting for the poet's journey back to his beloved's youth:

la sombra de las colinas de Meknès
sobre un campo de girasoles estáticos
es un golfo violeta.
Son las tres de la tarde,
tienes nueve años y te has adormecido
entre los brazos frescos de la rubia mimosa.[1] (AA:164–5; OP2:175)

(The shadows of the Meknès hills / over a field of motionless sunflowers / are a gulf of violet. / It is three in the afternoon, / you are nine years old and you are slumbering / in the cool arms of the fair mimosa.)

The scene, illuminated by an immense 'immobile sun' is entirely static except for the passage of the word, the song, from silence to silence:

... el canto del muecín
que perfora el silencio, asciende y florece
en otro silencio. (AA:165; OP2:175)

(the muezzin's chant / piercing the silence, rises and flourishes / in another silence)

This is the word as time, a central theme of *Blanco*. It is also the word as an invitation to the 'tú' who can set the scene in motion, an invitation to action and discovery:

Déjate llevar por esas palabras
hacia ti misma. (AA:165; OP2:175)

(Let those words carry you / towards yourself.)

Love is the force which can spur this action. The awakening of the sleeping soul through love is one of the most ancient motifs of imaginative literature and folklore. At the risk of sounding trite, we may call it the Sleeping Beauty motif.

The second section of the poem begins with a fundamental truth of the science of discourse: words say us as much as we say them. There follows a description of the word 'love' through the definitions and pronouncements of various authors and authorities. As noun it is a 'fatal espejo' in which the image of the beloved drowns in its own reflection, but as verb it is an appearance, an incarnation of identity:

> Aparición:
> el instante tiene cuerpo y ojos,
> me mira.
> Al fin la vida tiene cara y nombre.
> Amar:
> hacer de un alma un cuerpo,
> hacer de un cuerpo un alma,
> hacer un tú de una presencia. (AA:167–8; OP2:177)

(Apparition: / the moment has a body and eyes, / it looks at me. / Finally, life has a face and a name. / To love: / turn a soul into body, / turn a body into a soul, / turn a presence into a you.)

The act of love is what establishes the communication between a 'tú' and a 'yo' as a contact of identities, and it is what allows us to open the forbidden door to the other shore and transcendence, to our moment of 'fragile eternity.' Love is a mortal leap out of ourselves into communion, into existence, into immanence and mortality:

> amar es despeñarse:
> caer interminablemente,
> nuestra pareja
> es nuestro abismo. (AA:168; OP2:177)

(to love is to fall headlong: / fall unendingly, / our partnership / is our abyss.)

This is what archetypal psychology calls 'soul-making,' and Jung stresses that soul can live only in human relationships, to which the individual conscious of having achieved inner unity desperately clings.[2] The leap of love is precisely a leap into mortality because, as James Hillman explains, the soul's one certainty is death, just as its desire is immortality (1978, p. 280).

Just as the word is figuration, love is transfiguration:

Invención, transfiguración:
la muchacha convertida en fuente,
la cabellera en constelación,
en isla la mujer dormida. (AA:169; OP2:178)

(Invention, transfiguration: / the girl turned into a fountain, / her hair into a constellation, / the sleeping woman into an island.)

It is the synesthetic transformation of sensation into music, of touch into light, the transgression of natural law, the point of union between freedom and destiny, a poetic act. Poetry, in fact, is the point of contact (the unifying principle) between Paz's quest for personal development and individuation and his present conviction that this can happen only in amorous union with the other:

... sed de presencia,
querencia
de la mitad perdida.
El Uno
es el prisionero de sí mismo,
es,
solamente es,
no tiene memoria,
no tiene cicatriz:
amar es dos,
siempre dos. (AA:170; OP2:178)

(thirst for presence, / longing / for our lost half. / The One / is the prisoner of himself, / he exists, / he just exists, / he has no memory, / he has no scar: / love is two, / always two.)

Briefly, the soul is symbol (1978, p. 23) and love its symbolic act. The discourse of the symbol is a ritual of communion, and poetry is its most developed expression.

The third section of the poem is a meditation upon death. Love, the poet tells us, is a timeless island surrounded by time, a clarity surrounded by darkness, a union of polarities, a synthesis of paradox. It is in this vein that we may understand that love's very acceptance of mortality is its joyous consciousness of the great circle of life. The poet asks

El arte de amar
¿es arte de morir? (AA:171; OP2:179)

(The art of loving / is the art of dying?)

And he answers

Amar
es morir y revivir y remorir:
es la vivacidad.
Te quiero
porque yo soy mortal
y tú lo eres. (AA:171; OP2:179)

(To love / is to die and live again and die again: / it is life energy. / I love you / because I am mortal / and you are too.)

Finally, it is 'reconciliación con el Gran todo / y con los otros.' It is an expression of the 'fraternidad cósmica,' which is the term Paz uses in *La otra voz* (1990) to describe poetry: 'A mirror of cosmic fraternity, the poem is a model of what human society could be. In the face of the destruction of nature, it reveals the brotherhood of stars and particles, chemical substances and conscience. Poetry exercises our imagination and thereby trains us to recognize differences and discover similarities. The universe is a living texture of contrasts and affinities. A living proof of universal brotherhood, every poem is a practical lesson in harmony and concord' ... Poetry is the antidote to technology and the market. This, then, is what the function of poetry might be in our time, and in the time that is coming. Nothing more? Nothing less.'[3] This conception is both Utopian and Platonic, as is revealed in the correspondence between the writing in the stars, the single Word, and the plurality of mortal names we write here below, pure form on the one hand, and multiple manifestation on the other:

En la altura
las constelaciones escriben siempre
la misma palabra;
nosotros,
aquí abajo, escribimos
nuestros nombres mortales. (AA:173; OP2:180)

(Up on high / the constellations always write / the same word; / we, / here below, write / our mortal names.)

It is an idealistic conception of the world, but not a regression to a lost paradise. Though we are condemned as human beings to try and invent the Garden of Eden, cultivating delirious fantasies of the world 'as it should be,' we are in the last analysis condemned to leave the Garden and walk into the world:

Estamos condenados
a dejar el Jardín:
delante de nosotros
está el mundo. (AA:173; OP2:180)

(We are condemned / to leave the Garden: / before us / is the world)

In the concentrated verses of the coda, this thought is completed. Love is commitment to this world and learning to walk in it. It is also the lesson of serenity and of vision, the acceptance of the self as the process of development of the other. The modern Eve does not pluck a fruit from the tree of knowledge. She plants it. It is the tree inside and outside the self: there is no difference. And Adam, the poet, realizes that he speaks only because her spirit sways the leaves and branches.

Conclusions
A Handful of Words

In our brief study, we hope to have shown how the life and work of Octavio Paz have, through multiple circularities, come full circle. His last creative phase can be seen, in its simplicity and true to Paz's style, as much a beginning as an end, but an end it certainly is, in the sense of a culmination. The purpose of the dialogue we attempted to set up between the discourse of two revolutionary and creative minds of the twentieth century, the resonances we have sought to establish between the words and images of the two, despite their focus on very different subjects, was to reveal something of both Octavio Paz the poet and Octavio Paz the man.

We tried to show how, in the enormous development of Octavio Paz's first creative phase, from youthful enthusiast of the world of letters to professional poet, Jung's concept of the archetype and his description of common archetypal motifs can illuminate the essential process of dialogue which Paz saw as the business of poetry – a dialogue with the other and with himself through a dialogue between the conscious mind and the unconscious.

Thereafter, we emphasized Jung's conception of the psychical importance of the mandala as essential to explaining the importance of this motif in most of the longer poems written by Paz, above all, *Piedra de sol* and *Blanco.* In so doing we went beyond Paz's own explicit definition of the term, as an eastern sacred figurative form, to look at its inner, psychological significance as a mental cosmos of integration and of the self. Thus, we were able to show that *Piedra de sol*, apart from being a Mexican poet's disquisition on Mexican culture, history, and time, is also a figuration of the emergence of the conscious ego and of the ensuing battle to establish the broader reality of the self and its place in the world.

Blanco, in turn, is a universal construct of the journey of the self and existence, a self-containing mandala, through language. In the true spirit of mandalas, it is a synthesis of the personal and the collective through poetry, in that it is a poem of poems written by an individual but offered to every reader as their poem, the Poem. Clearly, it is a watershed, given the full realization of the existential importance of language to which Paz now attains, which sets the course for all his future poetry. It is the pivotal point of the five phases of psychical-creative evolution, the midpoint between youthful development and maturity, and Jungian thought has enabled us to delineate it as such. As we have seen, Jung and Jungians speak of the two halves of the life cycle in psychological terms, the first concerned with the birth of the ego, the second with the integration of the self.

The latter phases of his creative development are seen by Paz himself very much as a return, not merely because of the biographical fact of his return to his native Mexico after years of living abroad, but a psychological and personal return to the source. The circularity of the development of the psyche and of creative genius is a characteristic which both Paz and Jung clearly perceived, which constitutes a profound area of resonance between their respective systems of thought. This circularity explains, in our view, how Paz's poetry revolves in constantly evolving and novel fashion around the same existential questions and images. Water, woman, fountain, stone, tree, light, among other basic natural images, are constants in Paz's poetry, but their significance is new at every turn. Paz's work does not leave behind past territories and memories in a linear evolution; it revisits them repeatedly as he gradually constructs for us, in a great cycle of cycles, the portrait of his being. His major work, his overall work, his completed work.

It may seem strange to some readers that, in attempting to establish a dialogue between Jung and Paz, we did not, in most cases, refer directly to the ideas of each, but brought them into contact through an exegesis of Paz's poetry, as well as the exegesis that Jung offers us of his patients' dreams. This is because the thought of each is an eminently figurative thought, focused through images, focused in each case on the symbols of mankind. In this respect, the importance of alchemy in the work of Jung can hardly be overstressed. In the mystical imagery that the alchemists applied to the physical process of creating the *lapis*, the philosopher's stone, Jung found particularly apt and pure illustrations of unconscious processes and the archetypal motifs of his depth psychology. Alchemy and dream content lived in constant creative interaction as the materials of his analysis. The significance of the treatises of the great alchemists of the past, largely forgotten in modern times along with their names, does not lie, then, in the physical process of blending elements that they purportedly describe. It is the amazing psychological portrait they give of their own unconscious mind and of the human unconscious in general. In that way, no modern description of chemical processes could be as half as interesting as theirs. And no one has described their work as richly and comprehensively as Carl Jung.

Unlike many applications of Jungian analysis to works of literature, which tend to concentrate on dream analysis and the major archetypal motifs of the process of individuation, we included Jung's alchemical studies as a major point of reference, looking not only at individuation, but also the *coniunctio*. For Paz, too, the *coniunctio* is an essential process: the binding together of opposites through words, and of the male and the female in the human soul. By showing similarities of words and images between Paz's poetry and alchemical treatises remote from him in time, place, and interest, we hope to have shown just how universal and generally human Paz's poetic images and processes are. Through the remarkable coincidences between texts which, in principle, should have no relevance to each other, we hope to have demonstrated the interaction of consciousness and the unconscious, the psychic processes at work in Paz's poetic texts. Thus, like all explorations of meaning, our 'dialogue' has been, in essence, intertextual.

Carl Jung, through his depth psychology of collective archetypes, was able to show, in the myriad varieties of symbolic thought throughout the world, the same recurring motifs and universal forms, the same creative quest for self and for conscious identity, born out of the undifferentiated realm of the unconscious. In the individual progress of the self, the cycle of psychic birth, death, and rebirth is continually repeated. Just as the individual is condemned to endlessly repeat his creative quest, the circular quest of the soul, so it may be that the poet is condemned to endlessly write the same poem. Each time the particularities are different, moving from the aesthetic dimension to the mythical, to the ritual and philosophical, and finally to the personal, as our commentary on Paz's five phases attempted to demonstrate. Yet the same search for harmony, integration, and the light at the centre is evident in each of Paz's major landmark poems. The ideas of Carl Jung illuminate for us a particular reading of them, a particular reading of their universality.

From Paz's fertile mind and active pen flowed, throughout his life, a vast range of writings in different genres and disciplines, on the most varied topics. Never shrinking from controversy or the conviction of his ideas, he was art critic and historian, literary critic, social commentator, anthropologist, structuralist, surrealist and orientalist. Concerns of the intellect were ever present in all of his writings, including his poetry. Even in the figures of poetry, he never feared to think out loud or to speak his mind. It is in this sense, not some facile self-ingratiating sense, that we must concur with Enrique Krauze's judgment: 'He was the greatest, and the most generous of Mexican writers' (1998, p. 7).

The thinking process gives his poetical works a sometimes erudite, sometimes hermetic or esoteric tone. Yet it is striking how, in the last decade of his life and in his last book of poetry, he laid aside the complexities of his vast learning, keeping only a handful of essential and intense words, daring to be simply a man. Sheridan recalls, in the 1997 interview conducted just a few months before the poet's death, a comment by Paz to the effect that the great poets of antiquity live among us 'thanks to a handful of syllables' (2004, p. 501). Octavio Paz, at the last, stood before us with a handful of words, conscious of his mortality, simply a man. But as he stood there in the night, alone, looking up and observing the vastness of sky, he also knew that there is writing in the stars. Deep in his heart of hearts, the depths of his unconscious mind, he knew that through his poetry he was part of the universe. That is the sense of what is fast becoming his most quoted poem:

Soy hombre: duro poco
Y es enorme la noche.
Pero miro hacia arriba:
Las estrellas escriben.
Sin entender comprendo:
También soy escritura
Y en este mismo instante
Alguien me deletrea.
(AA:37; OP2:112)

I am a man: I last but little
And the night is so vast.
But I look upwards:
There is writing in the stars.
I see without fully understanding:
I too am writing
And at this same instant
Someone is spelling out my words.

The life of Octavio Paz was dedicated to the defence and preservation of meaning in the modern world. That was the sense of his poetic task, the motive which informed his vision of poetry and his moral vision. The confidence that underlay that vision was the conviction that we are such stuff as words are made of, that as human beings our lives are part of the great text of the world.

Notes

Prelude

1 This point has been made by Octavio Paz on many occasions, both in his writings and in interviews. It is of such an essential nature that any specific reference or quotation would be merely pedantic.

2 Fortunately enough, there are alternative ways of characterizing post-modernism. Hillman, in *Archetypal Psychology*, speaks of 'the polytheistic structure of a post-modern consciousness' (p. 54), thereby recuperating myth as a central, informing source for pluralistic consciousness and perspectivalism. Possibly, postmodernism's major function is to 'problematize,' to borrow the inelegant term used by Linda Hutcheon in *A Poetics of Postmodernism.*

3 The distinction between the personal and collective levels of the unconscious is implicit, though not generally clearly expressed, in other currents of psychoanalysis. Kugler (1982, p. 48) points out that Lacan's dichotomy of symbolic and imaginary orders is analogous to this distinction.

4 The translation into English, as in all other instances of translation throughout this book, unless otherwise specified, is ours. See our remarks on the purposes of the English translations in the penultimate paragraph of this Prelude. The original citation in Spanish runs thus: 'La teoría de Platón sobre las reminiscencias y los arquetipos, singular anticipación de la doctrina del inconsciente colectivo de Jung, ¿no es acaso la primera y ya afortunada tentativa para explicar los mitos de los poetas, no como simples mentiras sino como verdades ocultas, como figuradas expresiones de la memoria inconsciente y sobrepersonal?' (Paz, 1988, p. 331).

5 It would seem, in fact, that Paz found little motivation to go to the sources of psychoanalytic thought directly, and that his allusions to both Jung and Freud arise indirectly through the intermediary of other works which have a

major influence on him, such as Roger Caillois's *Le mythe et l'homme.* Brief allusions to Jung, and more numerous, often critical references to Freud continue in Paz's later more famous essays on the poetic phenomenon, notably *El arco y la lira* (1956), after which they become more infrequent but occur as late as *La otra voz* (1990).

6 Our translation of Paz's somewhat more general formulation: 'esta sed de transformar lo instintivo en lo sobrenatural y de satisfacer, disfrazándolos en lo maravilloso, los más oscuros apetitos' (p. 273).

7 Our translation. The original text reads as follows: 'No ha desaparecido la necesidad de los mitos; sólo ha habido un cambio en la conciencia de los hombres y la zona psíquica de la credulidad imaginativa ... El hombre no es menos crédulo que cuando creía en la metamorfosis, sólo que ahora cree de otro modo y en otras cosas. Y si es cierto que el hombre ha conservado intacta su credulidad y su necesidad de mitos, aunque ahora se les designe con otro nombre, no lo es menos que aún posee la imaginación necesaria para crearlos y entenderlos. Trataré de exponer cómo la poesía, esto es, la imaginación creadora, ha producido siempre mitos para satisfacer esta sed de proyectarse en lo sobrenatural que el hombre padece. Y para esto, habrá que insistir y delimitar un poco en el significado de la palabra mito. Otro tanto debo decir de la palabra poesía' (1988, p. 273).

8 As Anthony Storr points out, 'Intuition is concerned with time. The intuitive person is able to 'see round corners,' to have hunches about things, and is more interested in the possibilities of things than in their present existence' (1973, p. 76).

9 'Poesía de soledad y poesía de comunión' is, for example, the title of a major 1943 essay, published in *Primeras letras* (1988, pp. 291–303).

10 Our translation of the original: 'En la comunión que el poeta busca descubre la fuerza secreta del mundo ... ¿Habrá que decir que esa fuerza, alternativamente sagrada o maldita, es la del éxtasis, la del vértigo, que brota como una fascinación en la cima del contacto carnal o espiritual? En lo alto de ese contacto y en la profundidad de ese vértigo el hombre y la mujer tocan lo absoluto, el reino en donde los contrarios se reconcilian y la vida y la muerte pactan en unos labios que se funden. El cuerpo y el alma, en ese instante, son lo mismo y la piel es como una nueva conciencia, conciencia de lo infinito, vertida hacia lo infinito ... El tacto y todos los sentidos dejan de servir al placer o al conocimiento; cesan de ser personales; *se extienden,* por decirlo así, y lejos de constituir las antenas, los instrumentos de la conciencia, la disuelven en lo absoluto, la reintegran a la energía original' ('Poesía de soledad,' 1988, p. 296).

11 The translation is ours; the original text runs as follows: 'lo que quería

hacer como escritor es *obras*, no simplemente explosiones verbales, sino obras con una estructura, con una intención, con una dirección' (Sheridan 2004, p. 500).

12 The original text reads as follows: 'No sé el valor de esos poemas, pero sí representan tres momentos de mi vida. Agregaría otro más, que escribí después: *Carta de creencia*. De modo que serían cuatro poemas. Me gusta el número cuatro porque alude a los cuatro horizontes, a los puntos cardinales. Es una figura geométrica muy querida por los antiguos mesoamericanos y que tiene un punto en el centro. Nunca son dos, sino cuatro soles, y en el centro, el sol del movimiento. El sol del movimiento podría ser en este caso el instante, el instante poético, los poemas cortos' (Tajonar 1998, p. 21).

13 The original Spanish text of our quotation is as follows: '"Blanco" es el poema más ambicioso que ha creado Octavio Paz, si no el más importante. Se trata de uno de los cinco brazos – junto con *Piedra de sol* (1957), *Nocturno de San Ildefonso* (1974), *Pasado en claro* (1974) y *Carta de creencia* (1987) – del delta de cinco grandes poemas en su obra' (Santí 1997, p. 301). More recently, Manuel Ulacia (1999) has invoked five stages in Paz's creative development, based more on his travels and activities than his poetic texts, and Tanius Karam (2005) also divides Octavio Paz's career into five stages, but again based on works and circumstances other than his poetry.

Phase One. *Libertad bajo palabra*: The Dialogue with the Other

1 The wealth of fascinating detail on Paz's childhood and youth whets the reader's appetite for a continuation of this biography beyond the 1960s, something that would connect the first part of the book to the final 1997 interview.

2 It is in this light, we think, that the combative, iconoclastic and revolutionary tone of some of Paz's statements and poems about surrealism should be interpreted. Where surrealism is a battle cry, it is a cry to do battle with words, words as doors to the unconscious and thence to a new conscious clarity. This aspect of surrealism, apart from the obvious illustrations in the poetry of the period we are examining, is summarized in a poem written years later in 1974, 'Esto y esto y esto,' published in *Árbol adentro* (p. 54) and republished as late as 2003 in the volume of the journal *Artes de México* devoted to 'México en el surrealismo,' p. 8.

3 The later, full version of *Libertad bajo palabra* includes *Bajo tu clara sombra*, *Calamidades y milagros*, *Semillas para un himno*, and *¿Aguila o sol?* as four numbered sections (cardinal points?) leading up to the fifth, *La estación violenta*, which culminates in *Piedra de sol*.

4 The text in Spanish reads: 'El surrealismo – en lo que tiene de mejor y más valioso – seguirá siendo una invitación y un signo; una invitación a la aventura interior y al redescubrimiento de nosotros mismos' (1971b, p. 183).

5 Paz is conscious, though, of the fact that this trend belongs to the Breton of the First Manifesto. In a 1953 interview he casts doubt on the currency of many of Breton's ideas from the early period: 'No creo que Breton actualmente haga suyas muchas de las afirmaciones de la primera época, fundadas en una interpretación puramente sicológica del hombre' (quoted by Wilson, 1980, p. 36).

6 This quotation and all successive ones from the prologue to *Libertad bajo palabra* can be found in SB:17–18 and OP1:23.

7 The archetypal symbol of the pre-conscious, undifferentiated state, represented always as a circular form, and typically as 'the circular snake, the primal dragon of the beginning that bites its own tail, the self-begetting *Ουρόβοροζ*' (Neumann 1954, p. 10).

8 The original text in Spanish is 'A todos, en algún momento, se nos ha revelado nuestra existencia como algo particular, intransferible y precioso. Casi siempre esta revelación se sitúa en la adolescencia. El descubrimiento de nosotros mismos se manifiesta como un sabernos solos; entre el mundo y nosotros se abre una impalpable, transparente muralla: la de nuestra conciencia. Es cierto que apenas nacemos nos sentimos solos; pero niños y adultos pueden trascender su soledad y olvidarse de sí mismos a través de juego o trabajo. En cambio, el adolescente, vacilante entre la infancia y la juventud, queda suspenso un instante ante la infinita riqueza del mundo. El adolescente se asombra de ser. Y al pasmo sucede la reflexión: inclinado sobre el río de su conciencia se pregunta si ese rostro que aflora lentamente del fondo, deformado por el agua, es el suyo. La singularidad de ser – pura sensación en el niño – se transforma en problema y pregunta, en conciencia interrogante' (Paz 1959, p. 9).

9 In a similar vein Manuel Ulacia, quoting Paz's essays, refers to 'love, liberty and poetry' as the triple pillars of the surrealist movement (1999, p. 118). He goes on to indicate that the correspondences between them are an important point of principle in which Paz and Breton are united (p. 121).

10 Anthony Storr, in his introduction to Jung's thought, explains this identification in perhaps overly simplistic terms: 'It might be said that extraverts tend to become over-involved with objects, and therefore run the risk of losing their own identities as separate persons' (1973, p. 66).

11 'Pregunta,' in *Puerta condenada* is a case in point. With intertextual echoes ranging from Macbeth to Gilberto Owen, the 'yo' addresses a 'tú' who is

'dios o ángel, demonio' and, in the second stanza, 'tú que huyes / aborrecible hermano mío' (SB:66; OP1:64). And the poems of revolution and social protest in *Calamidades y milagros* are clearly not addressed to a feminine 'tú,' for example, 'Entre la piedra y la flor' (SB:92–9; OP1:86–92).

12 Hillman's term 're-visioning' would seem appropriate here. Paz's own term, perhaps more pessimistic in perspective, is 're-inventing' (see, again, the prologue to *Libertad bajo palabra*).

13 Published originally in 1936 as 'Traumsymbole des Individuationsprozesses,' this lecture was later revised by Jung and published in *Psychologie und Alchemie* (Zurich, 1944). This work appeared in English as Volume 12 of the collected works (1953a, 1968). We quote here from the paperback partial version published under the title *Dreams.*

14 See, for instance, the various techniques of repetition in 'Nocturno mar,' 'Nocturno en que nada se oye,' and 'Nocturno Rosa' (1953, pp. 47, 57, 59). To the first sonnet, moreover, we may compare Villaurrutia's 'Soneto de la esperanza,' where the same topic of suspension of movement appears, though treated in a different fashion. The major source on information of Villaurrutia's influence on Paz, both as a contemporary and member of the group of the *Contemporáneos,* is of course Paz's own study of Villaurrutia's life and work (1978). See also Ulacia (1999, pp. 34–6).

15 'Historia' with a capital H for Paz, to distinguish it from 'historia,' individual story.

16 Naturally, Jung in his writings mostly had occasion to refer to the *lapis* or philosopher's stone. M.-L. von Franz points out that 'the alchemical stone (the *lapis*) symbolizes something that can never be lost or dissolved, something eternal that some alchemists compared to the mystical experience of God within one's soul' (Jung et al. 1964, p. 226). However, von Franz also indicates that stones in general, particularly round ones, are symbols of the self: 'the self is symbolized with special frequency in the form of a stone, precious or otherwise' (p. 221).

17 For his clarification of the meaning of all of these associations, see Jung (1963, p. 295ff).

18 See, for instance, the section entitled 'The transformation of the King' (1963, p. 265ff).

19 This association is noted by, among other critics, Valdés (1986) in his commentary on the first (and last) six lines of the poem.

20 As, for instance, Carlos Fuentes relates in his video history of Spanish civilization, *El espejo enterrado,* in the second video of the series, 'La batalla de los dioses' (1991). The work also appeared in book form (1997).

Phase Two. *Piedra de sol*: The Birth of Ego Consciousness and the Search for Self

1 The program 'Arte precolombino' in Televisa's series *México en la obra de Octavio Paz* (1989).

2 Ibid., my translation of a transcription of the television interview. The text in Spanish runs thus: 'La historia de Mesoamérica puede verse no sólo como una sucesión de acontecimientos ... sino también como una inmensa y dramática ceremonia ritual. Por eso nos apasiona y nos fascina. El tema de esa ceremonia, repetida una y otra vez en todas las culturas y todas las épocas, es el mito del origen, la creación del mundo, la destrucción del mundo. Creación – destrucción, creación -destrucción, la idea central que anima a la civilización mesomericana. No la sucesión lineal de la historia de Occidente, sino más bien una visión mítica del acontecer humano. La historia se repite como se repiten los días y los años, las eras y los siglos, los planetas y las constelaciones. La historia de los hombres es un episodio de la historia de los astros y de las cosmologías.'

3 Translation ours. The original text in Spanish reads as follows: 'En la portada de este libro aparece la cifra 585 escrita con el sistema maya; asimismo los signos mexicanos correspondientes al Día 4 Olín (Movimiento) y el Día 4 Ehécatl (Viento) figuran al principio y al fin del poema. Quizá no sea inútil señalar que este poema está compuesto por 584 endecasílabos (los seis últimos no cuentan porque son idénticos a los seis primeros; en realidad con ellos no termina sino vuelve a empezar el poema). Este número de versos es igual al de la revolución sinódica del planeta Venus ... que es de 584 días. Los antiguos mexicanos llevaban la cuenta del ciclo venusino (y de los planetas visibles a simple vista) a partir del Día 4 Olin; el Día 4 Ehécatl señalaba 584 días después de la conjunción de Venus y el Sol y, en consecuencia, el fin de un ciclo y el principio de otro. El lector interesado puede encontrar más completa (y mejor) información sobre este asunto en los estudios que ha dedicado al tema el licenciado Raúl Noriega, a quien debo estos datos.

El planeta Venus aparece dos veces al día como Estrella de la Mañana (Phosphorus) y como Estrella de la Tarde (Hesperus). Esta dualidad (Lucifer y Vesper) no ha dejado de impresionar a los hombres de todas las civilizaciones, que han visto en ella un símbolo, una cifra o una encarnación de la ambigüedad esencial del universo. Así, Ehécatl, divinidad del viento, era una de las encarnaciones de Quetzalcóatl, la serpiente emplumada, que concentra las dos vertientes de la vida. Asociado a la Luna, a la humedad, al agua, a la vegetación naciente, a la muerte y resurrección de la naturaleza, para los antiguos mediterráneos el planeta Venus era un nudo de imágenes y fuerzas ambivalentes: Istar, la Dama del Sol, la Piedra Cónica, la Piedra sin Labrar (que recuerda al 'pedazo de madera sin pulir' del taoismo), Afrodita, la cuádruple Venus de Cicerón, la doble diosa de Pausanías, etc.' (quoted in the classic article by Pacheco 1974, p. 173).

4 Translation ours. The original text in French reads thus: 'À l'origine de tous les êtres, et même des dieux, les anciens Mexicains imaginaient un couple primordial, *Ometecuhtli*, 'le seigneur de la Dualité,' et *Omeciuatl*, 'la dame de la Dualité.' Ils résident au sommet du monde, dans le treizième ciel, 'là où l'air est très froid, délicat et glacé.' De leur fécondité éternelle sont nés tous les dieux et naissent tous les hommes. À l'époque où nous nous plaçons, ces deux grandes divinités étaient devenues quelque peu semblables à des rois qui règnent mais ne gouvernent pas' (Sonstelle 1955, p. 123).

5 'This circle that you see is the calendar / Which, in turning full circle, / Shows the days of the Saints / And when they should be celebrated. / Each makes one turn through the circle, / Each star there represents a day, / Each sun represents a space / Of thirty days or zodiac' (our translation).

6 In this appreciation, and with respect to what we see as the essential movement and unitary dynamism of the poem, we beg to differ from interpretations too closely based on individualistic psychological perspectives, such as Román-Odio (1996), who sees the poem as the product of a divided subject.

7 From the first page of an article, 'Mandalas,' published in *Du: Schweizerische Monatsschrift* (Zurich) 15, 4 (April 1955), reproduced in the appendix of Jung (1959a p. 387).

8 These are not the only processes identifiable with the mandala: several others can be discovered in Jung's own nine-point list of mandala qualities (1959a, p. 361). See also the concluding pages of our chapter on Phase 3: *Blanco*.

9 We should point out that most explicit reference to the mandala form by both Paz and his critics occurs in relation to the poem *Blanco* (see Román Odio 2000 for a specific study on the subject). Yet this is no doubt because *Blanco* is a mandala constructed by Paz himself, whereas in *Piedra de sol* he *refers* to one constructed by the Aztecs. What is important for our argument is to see all Paz's major poems (*Piedra de sol*, *Blanco*, *Vuelta*) as mandalas through their circular structure and in terms of the psychological significance of mandalas as revealed by Jung. As an example of such a perspective, I refer to Paz's comments in a 1987 interview with Enrico Mario Santí, published under the title 'Conversar es humano' and reproduced in Volume 15 of Paz's Collected Works, *Miscelánea III* (2003, pp. 542–3).

10 See, in particular, dreams 9 and 59 (1953a, pp. 104 and 203).

11 Translation ours. The original in French reads thus: 'Au centre de l'énorme

disque de pierre qu'on appelle le Calendrier aztèque, un symbole en forme de croix de Saint-André encadre le visage grimaçant du Soleil. Quatre petits disques l'accompagnent. Le tout se lit: *naui-ollin*, 'Quatre-Mouvement,' et c'est le nom de notre monde, 'le nôtre, celui où nous vivons, et qui fut aussi celui de Notre Seigneur de Tula, le Serpent à Plumes.' Le mot *ollin*, soit dit en passant, signifie à la fois 'mouvement' et 'tremblement de terre,' et c'est le nom d'un des vingt jours du calendrier sacré à Mexico. Notre univers est né le jour 'Quatre-Mouvement,' quand le Soleil a commencé à se déplacer dans les cieux, et il s'effondrera dans des tremblements de terre et des cataclysmes. Alors les monstres du crépuscule, les Tzitzimimé au masque squelettique qui sont tapis dans l'ombre à l'Occident, attendant leur heure, surgiront des ténèbres pour exterminer l'humanité' (1967, p. 7).

12 They have done so with vastly different results and perspectives; see, for instance, Phillips (1972), Fein (1986), Valdés (1986), and Carpenter (2001).

13 The image of the wings opening in the sky, obviously reminiscent of the Holy Spirit in the Christian tradition, is interesting and complex. Neumann reveals another layer of its significance in relation to the image of the dove and to the Great Mother archetype: 'She [the Great Mother] was mistress of the mountains and of wild animals. Snakes and underworld creatures were sacred to her, but birds, too, symbolized her presence. The dove especially was her attribute, and she still remained a dove-goddess, both as Aphrodite and as Mary (dove of the Holy Ghost)' (1954, p. 76).

14 Fein speaks of this and the following stanzas as a 'hymn in praise of the poet's beloved' (1986, p. 24). He gives no reason, however, for his sudden switch from universal interpretations of symbols to this individual and personal interpretation. While we would be the first to admit that in *Piedra de sol* virtually every line *might* be read in personal and autobiographical terms, the archetypal significance of the female figure described would seem to be undeniable.

15 The intertextual echoes of French poetry are at their clearest here with the allusion to one of Baudelaire's best-known poems, 'Correspondances,' which, at least at the beginning, presents the universal confrontation of humanity, nature and symbol which is also a basis for *Piedra de sol*:

> 'La Nature est un temple où de vivants piliers
> Laissent parfois sortir de confuses paroles;
> L'homme y passe à travers des forêts de symboles
> Qui l'observent avec des regards familiers.'

The question of intertextuality in *Piedra de sol* will not be dealt with extensively in this chapter, mainly because we take intertextuality to be an automatic characteristic of any poem, and because the universal tone and nature of this poem will no doubt evoke for each reader different subjective intertextual echoes. The subjective implication of the reader in the poem is, for Paz, more important by far than any objective evidence of explicit intertextuality.

16 We should remember that the Aztec god of the sun, Tonatiuh, was also associated with the god of fire and known as Huitzilopochtli: 'hummingbird-wizard.'

17 This is not to deny the evident sexual connotations of these images.

18 Despite our current common association of Melusina with the French tradition as Mélusine, Jung observes that she occurs as a motif in a broad range of traditions throughout the world, from India to North America, and, citing Grimm, points out that the legend as we know it is apparently of Celtic origin. It is clear, then, that as an archetypal anima figure, her manifestations in the popular imagination have much earlier and more primitive roots than those simply of medieval legend.

19 We should remember that the first person to characterize the psychological processes of introversion and extraversion, and the corresponding introverted and extraverted psychological types, was Carl Jung, in his 1921 study *Psychological Types* (Vol. 6 of his Collected Works).

20 The hermaphroditic figure, similar to Mercury, in *Piedra de sol* itself is Quetzalcoatl. Callan identifies this aspect of the Toltec-Aztec god (1977, p. 917).

21 The image of personal mortality here may well seem like an echo of T.S. Eliot, reminiscent of *The Love Song of J. Alfred Prufrock.*

22 In the images of the feather duster and bones we may see a passing reference to the birth of Huitzilopochtli, according to Aztec myth, from a ball of feathers.

23 Eliot is one of the main literary influences studied by Manuel Ulacia in his useful summary of Paz's life and literary influences up to the end of the 1960s (1999; see especially pp. 102–15). He underlines Eliot's influence on Paz in the latter's conscious use of colloquial language as a private language with almost sacred functions (pp. 109–10), which is surely what is at issue here.

24 An image of singular force, yet difficult to interpret. The reference seems to be to a psychic energy, which is ghostly because it is absent and only apparent. The verses in question run as follows: 'un rey fantasma rige tus latidos / y tu gesto final, tu dura máscara / labra sobre tu rostro cambiante.'

25 As Quetzalcoatl must do after his immolation on the funeral pyre. The 'yo' seems to take on quite clearly here the persona of Quetzalcoatl.

26 Huitzilopochtli-Tonatiuh, the sun and fire god, the god in the centre of the stone, is the son of Coatlicue. The son can also be seen as the *filius regis* or *filius philosophorum* of alchemy, as explained below.
27 Jung gives the following clarification: 'The Scaiolae, as the four parts, limbs, or emanations of the Anthropos, are the organs with which he actively intervenes in the world of appearances or by which he is connected with it ... Since the Scaiolae, as we have seen, are also psychic functions, these must be understood as manifestations or effluences of the One, the invisible Anthropos. As functions of consciousness, and particularly as imaginatio, speculatio, phantasia, and fides, they "intervene" and stimulate Melusina, the water-nixie, to change herself into human form' (1967, p. 176).
28 See Jung's footnote to the text: 'May be interpreted as the "time of perfection."'

Phase Three. *Blanco*: Mandala and the Ritual of Meaning

1 Manuel Ulacia describes *Blanco* as the culmination of a period starting with *Salamandra* (1999, p. 297).
2 We refer to the epilogue of Santí's edition of *Archivo Blanco* (1995, pp. 235–321), reproduced in *El acto de las palabras* (1997, pp. 301–67).
3 Written in 1964 and published in the second edition of *El arco y la lira*, prepared in Delhi in 1967.
4 See the 1967 essay 'La nueva analogía: poesía y tecnología' (1994, p. 301).
5 'Los signos en rotación' (1994, p. 255).
6 This is, of course, the time of literary experiments such as Cortázar's *Rayuela*, and Umberto Eco's famous critical work *La opera aperta*.
7 Translation ours. The original text reads as follows: 'La superficie sobre la que se inscriben los signos, sean éstos caracteres fonéticos o ideogramas, es el equivalente, o mejor dicho, la manifestación del tiempo que, simultáneamente, sostiene y consume la arquitectura verbal que es el poema. Esa arquitectura, por ser sonido, es tiempo y de ahí que, literalmente, el poema se haga y se deshaga frente a nosotros. Aquello que sostiene el poema es aquello mismo que lo devora: la sustancia de que está hecho es tiempo. La página y el rollo chino de escritura son móviles porque son metáforas del tiempo: espacio en movimiento que, como si fuese tiempo, se niega constantemente a sí mismo y así se reproduce. Temporalización de la página: el signo escrito no reposa sobre un espacio fijo, como es el caso de la pintura, sino sobre una superficie que, por ser una imagen del tiempo, *transcurre*' ('La nueva analogía,' p. 306).
8 Translation ours. The original text is as follows: 'Algo así como el viaje

inmóvil al que nos invita un rollo de pinturas y emblemas tántricos: si lo desenrollamos, se despliega ante nuestros ojos un ritual, una suerte de procesión o peregrinación hacia ¿dónde? El espacio fluye, engendra un texto, lo disipa – transcurre como si fuese tiempo' (SB:481). Page references to *Obra poética I* are not given in the case of *Blanco*, since in this edition the poem is reproduced on a set of unnumbered grey pages.

9 Our rather approximate translation of 'el hombre es un emisor de símbolos' (1994, p. 316).

10 See Benvéniste's classic 1970 essay on the formal apparatus of enunciation published in his *Problèmes de linguistique générale II* (1974), also available in English and Spanish translation.

11 In a particularly dense passage, Paz describes our modern office blocks, factories, and public monuments as 'centros de energía, monumentos de la voluntad, signos que irradian poder, no sentido' (1994, p. 303).

12 The idea of four mental faculties representing a totality and associated clearly with parts of the body is, of course, well rooted in western gnostic and alchemical tradition: see Jung's explanation of the concept of the Scaiolae, for example, in note 27 of the chapter on *Piedra de sol*. Paz's classification here, though, of the individual faculties involved is perhaps more reminiscent of Jung's own classification of (conscious) thinking and feeling and (unconscious) intuition and sensation (see the Prelude, above, and Jung's 1921 study *Psychological types* [1971]).

13 The whiteness and brilliance associated with the fifth and sixth chakras of the throat and forehead (speech and understanding) are of particular relevance to *Blanco* as an association of the poem's central colour and meaning with both the spoken and the written word.

14 Our translation; the original text runs as follows: 'A esta disposición de orden temporal y que es la forma que adopta el curso del poema: su discurso, corresponde otra, espacial: las distintas partes que lo componen están distribuidas como las regiones, los colores, los símbolos y las figuras de un mandala' (SB:481).

15 Our translation; the original text is as follows: 'Otra carta posterior (9 de febrero de 1967) a Díez-Canedo ... revela que al principio el autor pensó ponerle el título de *Sunyata*, "que quiere decir vacío o vacuidad y que, en el budismo mahayana, también quiere decir realidad – realidad de realidades: Samsara es igual a Nirvana, la realidad a la irrealidad, la locura a la sabiduría." Pero abandonado también ese primer título, opta por *Blanco*: "es el equivalente de *Sunyata* – inclusive en el sentido de que es un estado por definición inalcanzable, ese blanco que nunca tocamos"' (Santí 1997, p. 302).

16 Translation ours; the original text reads as follows: 'Es precisamente la conciencia de que el budismo se funda "en una teoría combinatoria del mundo y del ego que prefigura a la lógica contemporánea," como dice a continuación el mismo pasaje de *Claude Lévi-Strauss*, el paso decisivo que dará Paz en la comprensión de este pensamiento oriental; es decir, será el paso entre su primer encuentro con el budismo durante los años cincuenta y una década después. Tránsito del zen a la tendencia Madhyamika y, en particular, a su elaboración por Nagarjuna, 'su lógico' más célebre (150–250 a.C.) [*sic*; actually d.C.]. Si la máxima aspiración de la primera tendencia es la iluminación súbita (*satori o koan*), la otra en cambio postula algo mucho más radical: lo que revela el carácter fundamental de la relación no es otra cosa que el vacío, la impermanencia (*Sunyata*). El verdadero conocimiento, por tanto, no residirá ya en el triunfo de la paradoja sobre la lógica, o siquiera su consiguiente iluminación, sino en el vacío' (Santí 1997, p. 319).

17 Translation ours; the original text reads as follows: 'Con el término *vacio* el budismo Madhyamika (y en particular Nagarjuna) no quiso decir que nada existe (que es como interpretaríamos el concepto en Occidente), sino otra verdad: que todo es relativo. En efecto, en un primer momento al menos, la tendencia Madhyamika es relativista, ya que concibe las cosas desprovistas de lo que el budismo llama *svabhava*, 'propio ser.' Como nada tiene sustancia independiente o eterna, las cosas, siendo imágenes de sueño o ilusión, ni existen sustancialmente ni dejan de existir absolutamente' (Santí 1997, pp. 319–20).

18 Translation ours; the original text reads as follows: 'La esencia de la palabra es la relación y de ahí que sea la cifra, la encarnación monentánea de todo lo que es relativo. Toda palabra engendra una palabra que la contradice, toda palabra es relación entre una negación y una afirmación. Relación es atar alteridades, no resolución de contradicciones. Por eso el lenguaje es el reino de la dialéctica que sin cesar se destruye y renace sólo para morir. El lenguaje es dialéctica, operación, comunicación' (Paz 1996, p. 557).

19 In Paz's words: 'la posibilidad de combinar dos elementos contradictorios: la extensión y la intensidad, la concentración y la sucesión, lo que pasa aquí y lo que pasa allá' (note to the first edition of *Blanco*, quoted in Santí 1997, p. 313).

20 Translation ours; the original text reads as follows: 'Por lo pronto, debemos reconocer que la observación va más allá del mero dato sobre teoría literaria, o de lo que un crítico español, comentando la poética de la obra abierta, cierta vez llamara "la hora del lector." Se trata más bien de una visión metafísica que reconoce la libertad de la lectura y que conmina al lector de la obra abierta a asumirla en todas sus dimensiones. "En la India – observa Paz en otro pasaje de *Corriente alterna* – la negación, no menos sutil que la de

Occidente aunque aplicada a otros fenómenos, está al servicio de la indeterminación; su oficio es abrirnos las puertas de lo incondicionado" (p. 141). Es decir, la indeterminación de la obra abierta apunta, en última instancia, a la indeterminación de la vida: el componente "incondicionado" que solemos conocer bajo los nombres de Azar, Suerte, Accidente, Aventura o Destino: formas de la *otredad.* Juego de la escritura, la obra abierta confronta al lector con su propia libertad' (Santí 1997, p. 313).

21 Translation ours; the original text reads: 'Ya dije mi creencia: el tiempo moderno, el tiempo lineal, homólogo de las ideas de progreso e historia, siempre lanzado hacia el futuro; el tiempo del signo *no-cuerpo,* empeñado en dominar a la naturaleza y domeñar a los instintos, el tiempo de la sublimación, la agresión y la automutilación: nuestro tiempo – se acaba ... El tiempo que vuelve, si es que efectivamente vivimos una vuelta de los tiempos, una revuelta general, no será ni un futuro ni un pasado sino un presente ... Tiempo carnal, tiempo mortal: *el presente no es inalcanzable, el presente no es un territorio prohibido* ... nuestros ojos incrédulos serán testigos del despertar y vuelta a nuestro abyecto mundo de esa realidad, corporal y espiritual, que llamamos 'presencia amada.' Entonces el amor dejará de ser la experiencia aislada de un individuo o una pareja, una excepción o un escándalo.'

22 See Jung's commentary on 'The secret of the golden flower' (1967, chap. 1). See also Román Odio's treatment of the flower image in *Blanco* (2000, pp. 507–9).

23 The theory of multimodality, with its central idea that every text or message is the product not of a single semiotic code but rather of a sum of different potential modes of expression, has developed in various theoretical currents since the 1990s. To our mind, the most cogent formulation, developing out of social semiotics (Hodge and Kress 1988) is that of Kress and van Leeuwen (2001), further developed in Kress (2003) and van Leeuwen (2005), among a rich series of other publications by these authors and their associates. This theory, which holds that a plurality of modes is a normal potential for every text, not only special works such as sacred, literary, or poetic texts, offers, in our opinion, a more satisfactory explanation of the semiotic of *Blanco* than the rhetorical theory of ekphrasis advanced by Román Odio (2000) in her commentary on the poem.

Phase Four. *Vuelta, Nocturno de San Ildefonso,* and *Pasado en claro:* The Circular Journey and Return to the Source

1 For readers not familiar with Mexican poetry, in his main poetic work *Simbad el varado,* Gilberto Owen takes on the persona of Sinbad the sailor, in a half-

ironic vein, since his Sinbad is cast up on dry land. This poem is, incidentally, the clearest example we know of the night sea voyage motif in Mexican literature, even if it is a figurative sea voyage rather than an actual one.

2 As Claudia Albarrán (1992, pp. 545–6) points out in her commentary on the poem, these terms must be read in the context of modern Mexican colloquial speech. 'Coyote' and 'zopilote' have specific connotations in the bureaucratic society of modern Mexico.

Phase Five. *Carta de creencia*: The Human Couple

1 The phrase 'la rubia mimosa' is, incidentally, a perfect example of syntactic, linguistic fusion of the symbols of tree and woman, since it can be read as a description of a fair-haired woman or a mimosa tree. Could language here be functioning as a reflection of unconscious processes?

2 Quoted from Jung's *The Practice of Psychotherapy* by Hillman in *The Myth of Analysis* (1978, p. 25), where the matter is developed in greater detail.

3 Translation ours; the original text reads as follows: 'Espejo de la fraternidad cósmica, el poema es un modelo de lo que podría ser la sociedad humana. Frente a la destrucción de la naturaleza, muestra la hermandad entre los astros y las partículas, las substancias químicas y la conciencia. La poesía ejercita nuestra imaginación y así nos enseña a reconocer las diferencias y a descubrir las semejanzas. El universo es un tejido vivo de afinidades y oposiciones. Prueba viviente de la fraternidad universal, cada poema es una lección práctica de armonía y de concordia ... La poesía es el antídoto de la técnica y del mercado. A esto se reduce lo que podría ser, en nuestro tiempo y en el que llega, la función de la poesía. ¿Nada más? Nada menos' (1990a, pp. 138–9).

References

Albarrán, Claudia (1992). Vuelta. *Revista Canadiense de Estudios Hispánicos, 16* (3), 535–50.

Alt, Franz (Ed.) (1983). *Das C.G. Jung Lesebuch.* Olten: Walter Verlag.

Barnaud, Nicolas (1602). Commentarium in quoddam Epitaphium Bononiae. In *Theatrum chemicum* (Vol. 3). Ursel.

Benvéniste, Emile (1966). *Problèmes de linguistique générale.* Paris: Gallimard.

– (1974). *Problèmes de linguistique générale II.* Paris: Gallimard.

Bernard, Judith (1967). Myth and structure in Octavio Paz's 'Piedra de sol,' *Symposium, 21*: 5–13.

Bhattacharyya, Narendra N. (1982). *History of the tantric religion: A historical, ritualistic and philosophical study.* New Delhi: Manohar.

Callan, Richard J. (1977). Some parallels between Octavio Paz and Carl Jung. *Hispania, 60* (4), 916–26.

Campbell, Joseph (1974). *The mythic image.* New York: MJF Books.

Carpenter, Victoria (2001). Dream-sex and time travel: The meaning of 'Piedra de sol' by Octavio Paz. *Bulletin of Hispanic Studies, 78* (4), 493–513.

Caso, Alfonso (1953). *El pueblo del sol.* Mexico: Fondo de Cultura Económica.

Castañón, Alfredo, et al. (1994). *Octavio Paz en sus 'Obras completas.'* Mexico: Consejo Nacional para la Cultura y las Artes & Fondo de Cultura Económica.

Chantikian, K. (Ed.). (1980). Homage to Octavio Paz [Special issue]. *Kosmos, 5–6.*

Chiles, Frances (1987). *Octavio Paz: The mythic dimension.* New York: Peter Lang.

Dehennin, Elsa (1973). Stone and water imagery in Paz's poetry. In Ivask (1973), pp. 97–105.

Durán, Manuel (1973). Irony and sympathy in *Blanco* and *Ladera este.* In Ivask (1973), pp. 67–74.

'El legado de Octavio Paz' (1998, 26 April). *La Jornada semanal, 164.* Homage to Octavio Paz with contributions by Baranda, Boullosa, Bracho, Buxó, Canpos, Castañón, Chaves, Chumacero, Deltoro, Domínguez, Fernández-Granados, Gutiérez Vega, Helguera, Hiriart, Huerta, Hurtado, Landa, Manjárrez, Masoliver, Mendiola, Milán, Monsiváis, Morábito, Moscona, Ortega, Poniatowska, Sada, Serrano, Ulacia, Valdés, and Volkow.

Fein, John A. (1986). *Toward Octavio Paz: A reading of his major poems.* Lexington: University Press of Kentucky.

Flores, Ángel (1974). *Aproximaciones a Octavio Paz.* Mexico: Joaquín Mortiz.

Fordham, Frieda (1953). *An introduction to Jung's psychology.* Harmondsworth, UK: Penguin.

Franco, Jean (1971). ¡Oh mundo por poblar, hoja en blanco! El espacio y los espacios en la obra de Octavio Paz. *Revista iberoamericana, 37* (74), 147–60.

Frazer, James (1993) [1922]. *The golden bough: A study in magic and religion.* Ware, UK: Wordsworth Editions.

Freud, Sigmund (1965). *The interpretation of dreams.* New York: Avon Books.

Fuentes, Carlos (1991). *El espejo enterrado* [Video series]. Mexico: Sogetel.

– (1997). *El espejo enterrado* [Book]. Mexico: Fondo de Cultura Económica

– (1998 10 May). Mi amigo Octavio Paz. *Los Angeles Times,* p. 6. Also published in *New Perspectives Quarterly, 15,* 4 (1998): 57–9. Spanish original published in *Reforma,* 6 May 1998, Seccione Cultura.

Gimferrer, Pere (1980). *Lecturas de Octavio Paz.* Barcelona: Ediciones Anagrama.

– (ed.) (1982). *Octavio Paz.* Madrid: Taurus.

Hillman, James (1970). Why 'archetypal psychology'? *Spring,* 212–19.

– (1975). *Re-visioning psychology.* New York: Harper & Row.

– (1978). *The myth of analysis.* New York: Harper Collins.

– (1983). *Archetypal psychology: A brief account.* Dallas: Spring.

Hodge, Robert, and Gunther Kress (1988). *Social semiotics.* Cambridge: Polity Press.

Homage to Octavio Paz [Special issue]. (1998, May). *Vuelta, 258.* Contributions by Aurelio Asiain, Enrique Krauze, Eduardo Lizalde, Gabriel Zaid, Pere Gimferrer, Francisco Serrano, Adolfo Castañón, Tulio Demicheli and Fabienne Bradu.

Hutcheon, Linda (1988). *A poetics of postmodernism: History, theory, fiction.* London: Routledge.

Ivask, Ivar (Ed.). (1973). *The perpetual present: The poetry and prose of Octavio Paz.* Norman: University of Oklahoma Press.

Jiménez Cataño, Rafael (1992). *Octavio Paz: Poética del hombre.* Pamplona: EUNSA.

Jung, Carl G. (1953a). *Psychology and alchemy.* Collected Works (Vol. 12). Princeton: Princeton University Press (2nd rev. ed. published 1968).
– (1953b). *Two essays on analytical psychology.* Collected Works (Vol. 7). Princeton: Princeton University Press.
– (1959a). *The archetypes and the collective unconscious.* Collected Works (Vol. 9, part 1). Princeton: Princeton University Press.
– (1959b). *Aion: Researches into the phenomenology of the self.* Collected Works (Vol. 9, part 2). Princeton: Princeton University Press.
– (1959c). *Four archetypes: Mother/rebirth/spirit/trickster.* Princeton: Princeton University Press.
– (1963). *Mysterium coniunctionis.* Collected Works (Vol. 14). Princeton: Princeton University Press.
– (1967). *Alchemical studies.* Collected Works (Vol. 13). Princeton: Princeton University Press.
– (1971). *Psychological types.* Collected Works (Vol. 6). Princeton: Princeton University Press.
– (1973). *Experimental researches.* Collected Works (Vol. 2). Princeton: Princeton University Press.
– (1974). *Dreams.* Princeton: Princeton University Press.
– (1984). *The spirit in man, art and literature.* Ark Paperbacks. London: Routledge.
– (1988). *On the nature of the psyche.* Ark Paperbacks. London: Routledge.
Jung, Carl G., et al. (1964). *Man and his symbols.* New York: Dell.
Karam, Tanius (2005). *Piedra del sol*: Un acercamiento comunicológico a la vida-obra de Octavio Paz. *Espéculo: Revista de estudios literarios, 29* (March–June). Assessed July 2005 from http://www.ucm.es/info/especulo/numero29/opazcomu.html.
King, Lloyd (1969). Surrealism and the sacred in the aesthetic credo of Octavio Paz. *Hispanic Review 37* (3), 383–93.
Krauze, Enrique (1998). El sol de Octavio Paz. *Vuelta, 258* (May), 7.
Kress, Gunther (2003). *Literacy in the new media age.* London: Routledge.
Kress, Gunther, & Theo van Leeuwen (2001). *Multimodal discourse: The modes and media of contemporary communication.* London: Arnold.
Kugler, Paul (1982). *The alchemy of discourse: An archetypal approach to language.* Lewisburg, PA: Bucknell University Press.
Lemaître, Monique J. (1976). *Octavio Paz: Poesía y poética.* Mexico: Universidad Nacional Autónoma de México.
Magis, Carlos H. (1978). *La poesía hermética de Octavio Paz.* Mexico: El Colegio de México.
Martínez Torrón, Diego (1979). *Variables poéticas de Octavio Paz.* Madrid: Hiperión.

Más, José L. (1980). Las claves estéticas de Octavio Paz en *Piedra de sol. Revista iberoamericana, 46*, 112–13.

México en el surrealismo: La transfusión creativa. (2003, April) *Artes de México, 64.*

Mora, Jorge A. (1978). *La divina pareja: Historia y mito en Octavio Paz.* Mexico: Ediciones Era.

Nelken, Zoila E. (1968). Los avatares del tiempo en 'Piedra de sol' de Octavio Paz. *Hispania, 51* (1), 92–4.

Neumann, Erich (1954). *The origins and history of consciousness.* Princeton: Bolingen Series 62. Princeton University Press.

Nugent, Robert (1966). Structure and meaning in Octavio Paz's 'Piedra de sol.' *Kentucky Foreign Language Quarterly, 13* (1), 138–46.

Octavio Paz 1914–1998. (1998). Homage in *Nexos* 245 (May), 77–85.

Ortega, José (1979). Tiempo y alienación en '*Piedra de sol.*' *Cuadernos hispanoamericanos, 343–5*, 437–44.

Pacheco, José Emilio (1974). Descripción de 'Piedra de sol.' In Flores (1974), 173–82.

Palau de Nemes, Graciela (1971). Blanco de Octavio Paz: Una mística espacialista. *Revista iberoamericana, 37* (74), 183–96.

Pastén B, Josë Agustín (1999). *Octavio Paz: Crítico practicante en busca de una poética.* Madrid: Pliegos.

Paz, Octavio (1937a). *Raíz del hombre.* Mexico: Simbad.

– (1937b). *Bajo tu clara sombra y otros poemas sobre España.* Valencia: Ediciones Españolas.

– (1949). *Libertad bajo palabra.* Mexico: Fondo de Cultura Económica.

– (1950). *El laberinto de la soledad* (1st ed.). Mexico: Fondo de Cultura Económica.

– (1951). *¿Águila o sol?* Mexico: Fondo de Cultura Económica.

– (1954). *Semillas para un himno.* Mexico: Fondo de Cultura Económica.

– (1956a). *El arco y la lira.* Mexico: Fondo de Cultura Económica.

– (1956b). *The bow and the lyre.* Translated by Ruth L.C. Simms. Austin: University of Texas Press.

– (1957). *Piedra de sol.* Mexico: Fondo de Cultura Económica.

– (1958). *La estación violenta.* Mexico: Fondo de Cultura Económica.

– (1959). *El laberinto de la soledad* (2nd ed., rev. and expanded). Mexico: Fondo de Cultura Económica (first published 1950).

– (1960). *Libertad bajo palabra.* Mexico: Fondo de Cultura Económica (2nd ed. 1968).

– (1961). *The labyrinth of solitude: Life and thought in Mexico* (Lysander Kemp, Trans.). New York: Grove Press, London: Evergreen Books.

– (1962). *Salamandra (1958–1961).* Mexico: Joaquín Mortiz.

– (1965a). *Los signos en rotación.* Buenos Aires: Sur.

– (1965b). *Cuadrivio.* Mexico: Joaquín Mortiz.
– (1965c). *Viento entero.* Delhi: Caxton Press.
– (1966). *Puertas al campo.* Barcelona: Seix Barral.
– (1967a). *Blanco.* Mexico: Joaquín Mortiz.
– (1967b). *Claude Lévi-Strauss o el nuevo festín de Esopo.* Mexico: Joaquín Mortiz.
– (1967c). *Corriente alterna.* Mexico: Siglo XXI.
– (1968). *Discos visuales.* Mexico: Ediciones Era.
– (1969a). *Ladera Este (1962–1968).* Mexico: Joaquín Mortiz.
– (1969b). *Conjunciones y disyunciones.* Mexico: Joaquín Mortiz.
– (1970). *Posdata.* Mexico: Siglo XXI.
– (1971a). *Topoemas.* Mexico: Ediciones Era.
– (1971b). *Las peras del olmo.* Barcelona: Seix Barral. (1st ed. UNAM, 1957.)
– (1971c). *Los signos en rotación y otros ensayos* (Carlos Fuentes, Ed. & Intro.). Madrid: Alianza.
– (1973). *El signo y el garabato.* Mexico: Joaquín Mortiz.
– (1974a). *Los hijos del limo: Del romanticismo a la vanguardia.* Barcelona: Seix Barral.
– (1974b). *El mono gramático.* Barcelona: Seix Barral.
– (1975). *Pasado en claro.* Mexico: Fondo de Cultura Económica.
– (1976). *Vuelta.* Mexico: Barcelona: Seix Barral.
– (1978). *Xavier Villaurrutia en persona y en obra.* Mexico: Fondo de Cultura Económica.
– (1979a). *Poemas (1935–1975).* Barcelona: Seix Barral.
– (1979b). *A draft of shadows and other poems* (Eliot Weinberger, Ed. & Trans.). New York: New Directions.
– (1979c). *El ogro filantrópico.* Mexico: Joaquín Mortiz.
– (1979d). *In/mediaciones.* Barcelona: Seix Barral.
– (1982). *Sor Juana Inés de la Cruz o las trampas de la fe.* Mexico: Fondo de Cultura Económica.
– (1984). *Hombres en su siglo y otros ensayos.* Barcelona: Seix Barral.
– (1985). *Pasión crítica.* Barcelona: Seix Barral.
– (1987a). *Árbol adentro.* Barcelona: Seix Barral.
– (1987b). *The collected poems of Octavio Paz, 1957–1987* (Eliot Weinberger, Ed. & Trans.). New York: New Directions.
– (1987c). *Generaciones y semblanzas: 3. Literatura contemporánea.* México en la obra de Octavio Paz 6. Mexico: Fondo de Cultura Económica.
– (1987d). *Los privilegios de la vista: I. Arte antiguo y moderno.* México en la obra de Octavio Paz 7. Mexico: Fondo de Cultura Económica.
– (1988). *Primeras letras (1931–1943)* (Enrico M. Santí, Ed.). Mexico: Ediciones Vuelta.

– (1990a). *La otra voz: Poesía y fin de siglo.* Barcelona: Seix Barral.

– (1990b). *In search of the present.* Nobel lecture 1990. Bilingual ed. San Diego: Harcourt Brace Jovanovich.

– (1993). *La llama doble: Amor y erotismo.* Barcelona: Seix Barral.

– (1994). *La casa de la presencia: Poesía e historia.* Obras completas (2nd ed., Vol. 1). Mexico: Fondo de Cultura Económica.

– (1995a) *Vislumbres de la India.* Barcelona: Seix Barral.

– (1995b). *Ideas y costumbres I: La letra y el cetro* Obras completas (2nd ed., Vol. 9). Mexico: Fondo de Cultura Económica.

– (1996). *Ideas y costumbres II: Usos y símbolos.* Obras completas (2nd ed., Vol. 10). Mexico: Fondo de Cultura Económica.

– (1997). *Obra poética I (1935–1970).* Obras completas (2nd ed., Vol. 11). Mexico: Fondo de Cultura Económica.

– (2003a). *Obra poética II (1969–1998).* Obras completas (2nd ed., Vol. 12). Mexico: Fondo de Cultura Económica.

– (2003b). *Miscelánea III: Entrevistas.* Obras completas (2nd ed., Vol. 15). Mexico: Fondo de Cultura Económica.

Paz, Octavio, & Tomlinson, Charles (1981). *Airborn / Hijos del aire.* London: Anvil Press Poetry.

Pezzoni, Enrique. (1972). Blanco: La respuesta al deseo. *Revista iberoamericana, 38* (78), 57–72.

Phillips, Rachel (1972). *The poetic modes of Octavio Paz.* London: Oxford University Press.

Pinho, Mario (1997). *Volver al ser: Un acercamiento a la poética de Octavio Paz.* New York: Peter Lang.

Poniatowska, Elena (1998). *Octavio Paz: Las palabras del árbol.* Barcelona: Plaza & Janés.

Poust, Alice (1979). Blanco: Energía de la palabra. *Cuadernos hispanoamericanos, 343–5*, 470–83.

Quiroga, José (1999). *Understanding Octavio Paz.* Columbia: University of South Carolina Press.

Rawson, Philip S. (1973). *Tantra: The Indian cult of ecstasy.* London: Thames & Hudson.

Ricoeur, Paul (1970). *Freud and philosophy: An essay on interpretation.* New Haven: Yale University Press.

Román Odio, Clara (1996). *Eros* retrospectivo / *Eros* visionario: El sujeto dividido de *Piedra de sol. Hispania, 79* (1), 28–35.

– (2000). Blanco: A western mandala. *Revista Canadiense de Estudios Hispánicos, 24* (3), 503–15.

Ruy Sánchez, Alberto (1990). *Una introducción a Octavio Paz.* Mexico: Joaquín Mortiz.

Santí, Enrico M. (1997). *El acto de las palabras: Estudios y diálogos con Octavio Paz.* Mexico: Fondo de Cultura Económica.

– (ed.) (1995). *Archivo Blanco.* Mexico: Ediciones El Equilibrista.

Saussure, Ferdinand de (1916). *Cours de linguistique générale.* Geneva: Multiple editions and translations.

Schärer-Nussberger, Maya (1989). *Octavio Paz: Trayectorias y visiones.* Mexico: Fondo de Cultura Económica.

Segovia, Tomás (1975). Poética y poema (por ejemplo en Octavio Paz). *Nueva Revista de Filología Hispánica, 24* (2), 528–40.

Séjourné, Laurette (1957). *Pensamiento y religión en el México antiguo.* Mexico: Fondo de Cultura Económica.

Sheridan, Guillermo (2004). *Poeta con paisaje: Ensayos sobre la vida de Octavio Paz.* Mexico: Ediciones Era.

Sinha, Indra (1995). *The great book of Tantra.* Rochester, VT: Destiny Books.

Slingerland, Adriana A. (1989). *Al reino de pronombres enlazados: búsqueda de la condición original a través de la imagen en* Libertad bajo palabra *de Octavio Paz.* Unpublished bachelor's thesis, Department of Latin-American Languages and Cultures (TCLA), University of Leiden.

Soustelle, Jacques (1955). *La vie quotidienne des Aztèques à la veille de la conquête espagnole.* Paris: Hachette.

– (1967). *Les quatre soleils.* Paris: Plon.

Stanton Anthony (1998). *Inventores de tradición: Ensayos sobre poesía mexicana moderna.* Mexico: El Colegio de México & Fondo de Cultura Económica.

– (ed.) (1998). *Correspondencia Alfonso Reyes / Octavio Paz (1939–1959).* Mexico: Fondo de Cultura Económica.

Storr, Anthony (1973). *Jung.* London: Fontana/Collins.

Tajonar, Héctor (1998). Interview with Octavio Paz. *La Jornada,* 26 April.

Ulacia, Manuel (1999). *El árbol milenario: Un recorrido por la obra de Octavio Paz.* Barcelona: Galaxia Gutenberg-Círculo de Lectores.

Underwood, Leticia I. (1992). *Octavio Paz and the language of poetry: A psycholinguistic approach.* New York: Peter Lang.

Valdés, Mario J. (1986). Comentario hermenéutico sobre la coda de *Piedra de sol. Actas del VIII Congreso de la Asociación Internacional de Hispanistas.* Madrid: Ediciones Istmo.

– (Ed.). (1992). Leyendo a Paz [Special issue]. *Revista Canadiense de Estudios Hispánicos, 6* (Spring).

van Leeuwen, Theo (2005). *Introducing social semiotics.* London: Routledge.

Verani, Hugo J. (1982). Octavio Paz and the language of space. *World Literature Today, 56* (4), 631.
– (1983). *Octavio Paz: Bibliografía crítica.* Mexico: Universidad Nacional Autónoma de México.
Villaurrutia, Xavier (1953). *Obras.* Mexico: Fondo de Cultura Económica.
Wilson, Jason (1980). *Octavio Paz: Un estudio de su poesía.* Bogotá: Ediciones Pluma (translation of *Octavio Paz: A study of his poetics.* Cambridge: Cambridge University Press).
Xirau, Ramón (1970). *Octavio Paz: El sentido de la palabra.* Mexico: Joaquín Mortiz.
– (1978). Octavio Paz y los caminos de la transferencia. In *Poesía y conocimiento: Borges, Lezama Lima, Octavio Paz.* Mexico: Joaquín Mortiz.
– (1993). *Poesía y conocimiento: Dos poetas y lo sagrado.* Mexico: El Colegio Nacional.

Index

[redacted]

FSC
www.fsc.org
MIX
Papier | Fördert gute Waldnutzung
FSC® C083411

Kolibri 360 GmbH
Ferdinand-Jühlke-Straße 7
99095 Erfurt, Deutschland
produktsicherheit@kolibri360.de